The Art & Truth of

Transformation For Women

*The Magic of Shifting Your Mindset
and Opening Your Heart
to Consciously Live a Life You Love*

Powerful You!
PUBLISHING
Sharing Wisdom ~ Shining Light

The Art & Truth of Transformation for Women

The Magic of Shifting Your Mindset and Opening Your Heart to Consciously Live a Life you Love

Copyright © 2020

All rights reserved. No part of this book may be reproduced by any mechanical, photographic, or electronic process, or in the form of a phonographic recording; nor may it be stored in a retrieval system, transmitted or otherwise copied for public or private use–other than for "fair use" as brief quotations embodied in articles and reviews–without prior written permission of the publisher.

The authors of this book do not dispense medical advice or prescribe the use of any technique as a form of treatment for physical, emotional, or medical problems without the advice of a physician, either directly or indirectly. Nor is this book intended to provide personalized legal, accounting, financial, or investment advice. Readers are encouraged to seek the counsel of competent professionals with regards to such matters. The intent of the authors is to provide general information to individuals who are taking positive steps in their lives for emotional and spiritual well-being. If you use any of the information in this book for yourself, which is your constitutional right, the authors and the publisher assume no responsibility for your actions.

Published by: Powerful You! Inc. USA
powerfulyoupublishing.com

Library of Congress Control Number:2020916845

Sue Urda and Kathy Fyler –First Edition

ISBN: 978-1-7356579-0-5

First Edition October 2020

Self Help / Personal Growth

Printed in the United States of America

Dedication

For you, a woman on the
evolutionary journey of
becoming and being yourself
in all your power and beauty.

Table of Contents

Foreword
Roe Couture DeSaro

*"We delight in the beauty of the butterfly, but rarely admit
the changes it has gone through to achieve that beauty."*
~ Maya Angelou

Everyone has a unique identity in the world and we as human beings are constantly going through changes.

I think of humans like butterflies going through silent transformations breaking open into our wings of change. And yet that silence becomes broken open with our stories, our journeys, and personal stages of life, spirituality, and growth. As we evolve, we have the choice to eloquently and courageously describe what's going on inside our hearts and minds and that gives us a chance to understand any shift that is taking place within us.

This book is based on so many impactful stories of women, who have gone through a transformation. I want you to think of them all like butterflies including yourself as you change with each chapter and open your wings to fly higher and farther as you get through the book. This is a support system—we are a support system for one another. The stories you are about to read show the art and truth of transformation when you consciously decide to live a life you love.

You will feel it in these stories as you become your own catalyst for change to discover what's possible inside your heart—discoveries so big they will become life altering, just like a caterpillar miraculously changes into a butterfly.

Life moves as you move. Life stays stuck if you stay stuck. You have the choice to open your wings.

As I write this during such a time of unrest and uncertainty with COVID-19 among us, knowing that our world as we knew it is turned upside down, I want to encourage you to keep flying. If you put your life on pause, it's time to press play. If you've slowed down, it's time to use the ground for propelling. Listen to your intuition and feel your emotions again. Your reflection during any time in life is a journey of your rediscovery over and over again. If you're asking yourself, *"What's next? Where do I go from here?"* That's a good thing. You are consciously, silently flapping your wings to find the silver lining in the clouds and using your wisdom to realize that circumstances always arrive but you have to be willing to take flight no matter what.

I am reminded of my lowest moment in my life. It came after some of my highest moments. My story is not one of rags to riches. I was successful at a young age; I have the pleasure of breaking several glass ceilings for a major Wall Street firm. Over the course of my career I achieved great success in different industries and capacities, however, one of two things always happened: I either self-sabotaged myself or a global crisis destroyed my success.

I am a 911 survivor and as my million-dollar business shortly fell thereafter, I was left with my life to begin anew again. The aftermath went further downhill as the financial crisis of '08 set in and for the first time in my life, I felt like closing my wings. I began to feel *"Why bother, no matter how successful I can become, I will either destroy it or some major world crisis will come and wipe it all out."*

I was so down, that I started to believe that the only reason I was successful was because I was manipulative and selfish. But then one-day, I made the conscious choice to look at my lessons as blessings and I was reminded that it was I who was responsible for my decisions. And my life suddenly took shape into the present moment. Ten years after 911, I realized, I didn't escape with the boats crossing the Hudson River to New Jersey, I stayed behind to look for family and friends. Suddenly, seeing the power and the will that I put other lives ahead of mine, I began to identify myself as a servant leader and not the monster that I was making myself out to be. I realized the gifts that God gave me and I took the emotional wall that I built to protect myself and walked around it. I shifted my mindset, opened my heart and found my power again and moved forward, this time finding my calling in life! All of it came though discovery and reflection.

The women that you will meet on their own journeys in this book also decided to move forward. And with a *no matter what attitude,* while each tale is different, the outcomes all share volumes of transformation that can open your mind and heart to new ventures for yourself.

We are all human beings like butterflies. We must be willing to fly again.

Women are at a turning point to tap into our highest potential. Today, we want more and we know there is more and we're not only going to go after it, we are going to seize it. This is an historic moment for us as women. We have a powerful opportunity to support one another and this book may very well be your beginning to break open again into your own potential for your life to make sense again as you dream bigger than you ever imagined before.

Make the shift in your mindset and open your heart towards your deepest desire and your pathway will become clear.

Sue Urda and Kathy Fyler deliver in this book with the most amazing stories of ordinary women like you and I, who can and will transform no matter what circumstances come our way or theirs.

Sue and Kathy have the knack for finding everyday women who have found their courage to be willing to expose their deepest vulnerabilities. Let these stories stir up the courage that lives within you to open your heart, shift your mindset, seek your truth, and become your own beautiful butterfly.

With love and peace,
Roe Couture DeSaro
Your Gutsy Gal Guide

Introduction
Sue Urda

When we gather in the name of creation
all things are multiplied.

Storytelling is an art and a calling—all the authors in this book will tell you this is so. There are those who came forth open and willing to go to the depths of their personal journeys and others who came to their stories "kicking and screaming"—even though they chose of their own volition to take part in it. Interestingly, those who fought themselves the hardest along the way leave this project grateful in the knowledge that they stepped more fully into their true selves and unleashed their hearts.

Often the simple act of stepping into the work itself is an intricate dance and becomes its own transformational journey.

And so herein lie the hearts of twenty incredible women. Some of them had no idea that they were writers until the title of this book and the opportunity to collaborate called to them. They were compelled to open to the truth of themselves and put it on paper. Now on the other side of the writing process, they will tell you that they put forth not only some little-shared "secrets" about themselves, but also the essence of their hearts and souls.

Other authors came to this project secure in their writing ability but had never written such deeply personal and heartfelt material—at least not when they were the subject.

Either way, each decided it was time to help someone else with her story. Many of them wanted to tell of the ecstasy of their transformation or the happy story of how difficult situations can work out beautifully, no matter the starting point. Others used the opening this book has created to "come out" to their families and friends for the first time and more deeply connect with them.

What they all discovered is that an energetic transformation occurs when one puts pen to paper (or fingers to the keypad) with the intent to reveal her truth. As you read each story in this book, you will find yourself feeling the very core of the emotion of the author, whether she is speaking of opening to her inborn gifts, the journey of emotional or physical healing, creating a business venture, or she is yet again in the throes of another transformation.

If you are drawn to the title of this book, you are undoubtedly ready for your own transformation. By opening the pages you have already taken a step towards your destination, and in the reading of them you will catapult yourself even further along your intentional path. Why? Because we are all connected, and your desire and willingness cannot help but propel you forward. The only question is will you go forth with ease?

If you are ready for transformation, I invite you to open yourself up as our authors did when they wrote their stories. The inception of any new project—your transformational journey, for example—carries with it the excitement, anticipation, and a sense of mystery for what is to be revealed. Participants feel their way through a project (i.e. this book) most likely the same way they do in many other aspects of their lives: some with the mastery of one who instinctively knows her way; others, tentatively and carefully waiting for specific instruction at every turn; and still others who playfully step in and flow easily with whatever comes along—never worrying, simply accepting what is.

In whatever way you choose to participate, so be it. We only ask that you carry on!

My wish for you is that you commit to be "all in" and in full receiving mode to whomever and whatever shows up. Transformation is not always be easy. It is always worth it.

With deep gratitude and love,
Sue Urda
Your Feel Good Gal

TRANSFORMATION
is a moment by moment
opportunity.

Be Gentle with Yourself.

Becoming
Ann Franzese

*"We are not a finished product. We are a fluid process,
not a fixed and static entity—a flowing river of change,
not a block of solid material." ~ Carl Rogers*

L ife unveils a path from the moment we are born, the path to *becoming* who we are meant to be, seeking and searching for that deeper inner purpose that allows us to walk as our authentic selves, share our gifts and talents for the betterment of all, and inspire others as they follow their own unique journey.

Growing up in the South, religion and family were two important pillars that helped shape my early years. I experienced my first life transition when the schools in my area were integrated. While politics were not discussed much in my home, values of inclusion and being kind to all were reinforced. So when it was proposed that I be among the white students bussed across town to a primarily black school, my family and I readily agreed. There were no biases or judgments, as "we accepted each person as an equal." That experience has shaped my view of equality, from a lens perspective that we can all learn and grow together. While this transition did result in some transformation, it was not painful.

I could not say the same for other transformative events in my life. One that created my drive for independence was the onset of my mother's mental illness. My parents were very young when I was born—Dad was twenty-one and Mom, just eighteen. They lived in married student housing on the campus of the college my father attended. He later worked as a traveling auditor and was gone much of the time, leaving her to care for my siblings and me. Her mental illness surfaced about the time my brother was born, and when doctors knew far less about diagnosis and treatment. As a child I watched her decline from a vibrant, happy young woman, Girl Scout leader and Avon lady, to one who suffered the devastating highs and lows of mania and depression. Her illness, and the ineffective medications she was prescribed, resulted in her inability to take care of herself, much less the rest of us. Witnessing this set the course of my journey. I knew that one day I would pursue life—including my career, relationships, and mental health—with passion; I would also need to help myself so that I could in turn help others, including my family.

My next major transition came after graduating from college, when I moved to Chicago armed with my degree and my determination to make it in the "real world." Big city, lots of jobs, right? Certainly, I could find the lucrative sales position I was seeking. Let me say that innocence and naivety have their blessings. Equipped with my car, five hundred dollars, and a place to stay for a few weeks, I set off on my first solo adult adventure. I hit the ground running and soon found part-time temporary work. I scoured the want ads and soon found myself dressed in my new business suit, standing in line amidst a sea of other job seekers looking to fill valet and housekeeping jobs at the Landmark hotel, The Chicago Hilton, and Towers. While this wasn't what I was looking for, I surmised that I could meet the key people during the interview process that might assist me in obtaining the coveted hotel sales job. After thirty minutes in line, I was taken to the personnel office, thinking "Yes! Here we go," only to learn that the last internal sales position had been filled. They would, however, consider me if one became available. Next question was, how fast can you type? That's when I found out I would have to first be a sales assistant—not an exciting prospect.

I was processing this disappointment when the interviewer said, "You can see from the long line of candidates outside that we could use some extra hands in personnel to help process the new hires."

Was I interested? This was good news, and very timely, as my five hundred dollars was dwindling fast. They also agreed to give me the flexibility to take other job interviews.

My hope restored, I again directed my efforts to seeking a full-time job and fortunately landed one just weeks later. I could now afford a place of my own (barely) and start my career path, and my life, in earnest.

Maya Angelou once said, "Do the best you can until you know better, then when you know better, do better." As I have learned, there will be situations when once you know better you might not try it again. Indeed, if I had known how difficult and painful my "Chicago adventure" would be I might never have embarked on it. The next several years would bring many highs and lows, both personally and professionally. Sales can be very stressful, especially 100% commission positions; I also struggled with the loneliness that comes with building a life in a new city, especially such a large one.

I was the oldest child in my family and my siblings were still growing up. My mom and dad had recently divorced and their lives were in turmoil. My friends were far away building their own lives and we didn't speak nearly as often as we would have liked. I also struggled financially. The rent of my three-hundred-square-foot furnished studio was three times what I had paid for a shared but spacious three-bedroom in a full amenity complex in Knoxville, Tennessee!

Those first two years were arduous and yet full of growth. I learned how to lean into client conversations and business development, which were both engaging and beneficial for long-lasting relationships and outcomes. I helped develop my team at work and continued to develop my skills with the help of likeminded colleagues who understood that each of our successes played into the success of a whole. My social network also expanded and provided fruitful opportunities, both for travel and to engage more fully with my adopted city. I learned to embrace the four seasons, even those cold gray months of Spring that still required wool pants and a warm coat, gloves, and hat. Eventually, I upgraded my new residence, one in which the four walls didn't close in on me and was in a neighborhood that was safe, close to work, and in the action. I also met and married my husband. Life was good! I had made it through the other side, with no idea that my most difficult transition and transformative transformation was yet to come.

It was some twenty years later. I had retired into graduate school and had a family I adored. We had built and were living in our dream house, enjoying a wonderful life filled with fun, laughter, great friends, and family.

I cannot recall the exact moment I realized it wasn't quite that way anymore, and hadn't been for some time. In retrospect, I can see what I couldn't back then—how and why my husband and I were on such different pages; how the dynamics of raising kids revealed our varying beliefs and values; how our hopes and dreams began to differ; and, most importantly, the shift in power that resulted from my staying home and him being the sole income earner. My voice on certain issues quieted while his stress levels rose, especially in 2008 when the economy took a downward dive. The lack of communication left us both feeling empty and frustrated and, instead of being team players, we dug in, each counting our losses and wins. I couldn't quite pinpoint the problem, much less the solution, and neither could my husband, or, apparently, the counselor we saw.

Finally, it came to the point where I felt I could not tread water anymore. For years I had rejected the thought of divorce, as it violated my most deeply held core value: the sanctity of marriage and family. I made the decision to be married in front of God—how could I selfishly take that away from my spouse and children and unravel the extended family we loved so much?

Armed with the little power I felt from my extensive sessions with my own therapist, I began to consider what the next forty years would and could look like. Thus began a most challenging and emotionally draining process, made worse by long bouts of litigation and negative energy that pulled apart our kids. The values that we once lived by no longer applied. With changed beliefs, the rules and our boundaries seemed up for grabs too. That unbinding has had long-term repercussions—including tears, fears, disappointments, and anger—that will always be a part of their life journey.

My greatest transformation came once I completed my first round of a three-year litigation process. I vividly remember noting that I needed to regain control of my life. I needed to find a way to use my gifts and talents that could be impactful and fruitful, rather than sitting and waiting for others to decide what I could or not do with my life. After reaching out to key supporters and understanding some possible pathways, I joined a yearlong coaching program and started my new journey. It kicked off on my birthday weekend, a powerful symbol for me. This program gave me the insight to navigate the grief and pain I had been holding inside. It reassured me of my abilities and allowed me to slowly find my voice again. One thing that was particularly helpful was being able to see how and why my spouse and I had been at odds. I realized I could use this newfound information and transformation to help clients drive the change and trajectory in their own lives, not just for their own benefit, but for those they love.

In the words of famed psychologist Abraham Maslow, "One can choose to go back toward safety or forward toward growth. Growth must be chosen again and again; fear must be overcome again and again."

I've seen and lived the truth of this quote countless times through-out my life and as a coach to others. I have also learned that there are two kinds of people: those who embrace and even seek change, and those who ask why they have to change, why can't they simply be. This difference in perspective impacts the way each views their options in life and therefore their outcomes. The *fear of movement* or *change* is rooted from a very fixed attachment to one's identity.

It's like, "If I'm not who I think I am, then who am I?" This perspective sees our identity as static, fixed, and unchanging. It presents itself as *being* versus *becoming*. A more evolved viewpoint includes identifying core features and characteristics of our attitude so that we continually create our lives, adapting and evolving to new and higher levels.

Our predominant worldview informs our sense of self—and of others. When we see identity, including our own, as fluid, we feel more empathetic and forgiving. In this flow of *becoming*, we are no longer rooted in the hardship of fear, insecurity, or concerns about failure; instead we see each mistake as an opportunity to learn and experiment again.

Just as an artist crafts their art, so might we look at life. Learning to live artfully has us see our lives as a process rooted in curiosity, open to inquiry and learning, and always receptive to new meaning. As mentioned earlier, today I can reflect back based on what I know now and see how my spouse and I got to that stagnant space. Our tendency to see one another as fixed, or *being,* eventually mired us in those roles and stopped the flow of our relationship. On the other hand, when two individuals, each devoted to their growth, engages one another, they can have a relationship that is transformative for both.

Becoming is a paradigm of personal evolution and participatory change. Embracing this paradigm has not only transformed my own life, it has enriched my client work. This work, which has continued to evolve with my understanding, is devoted to catalyzing and enabling others to see various perspectives and be open to explore, discover, adapt, and flow with their life changes, whether those changes came about by their choice or not.

ABOUT THE AUTHOR: Ann is a leading authority in helping others cultivate emotional intelligence and shift their thinking to open doors to new possibilities and dreams. She has over twenty years of experience in the corporate sector, specifically sales/sales management, performance, business and organizational development, team-building, leadership, and succession planning. She has served on non-profits boards, with roles in operations, capital campaigns, organizational design, and fundraising. In addition to degrees from the University of Tennessee and Northwestern University, Kellogg Graduate School of Management, Ann holds coaching certifications from International Coaching Federation, Institute of Professional Excellence in Coaching (IPEC), and CreatingWe Institute. Ann resides in the Chicago suburbs with her son and daughter.

Ann Franzese
Executive Coach
journeytosuccess.me
ann@journeytosuccess.me
847-975-0500

The Power of Consistency and Manifestation

Ashlee Tuck

It was surreal. There I was just twenty-two years old and standing in the middle of my own yoga studio. It had been a dream of mine for four long years, and one I held onto even when it seemed like it would never happen. This journey was filled with challenges and blessings that completely transformed my life.

When I graduated high school I decided to take a year to really think about what I wanted to do. My parents were not in a position to send me to college, and besides, I had never believed attending a four-year university was necessary to live a successful life. I certainly didn't think taking out enormous loans with no guarantee of a return was a very smart idea either. I began exploring other creative avenues that really sparked something in me, and that's when I dove deep into a self-study of yoga. I was first introduced to yoga when I was a young Girl Scout, but really fell in love with it in high school, where it was part of the physical education curriculum. My teacher, Mrs. Godfrey, was such an inspiration to me and I have practiced yoga ever since.

I continued working my full-time job at Home Depot while I considered my next steps. My mom was not supportive of my decisions and thought not going to college meant her child was "lazy." Despite this, I remained determined to continue down this new path. One evening I Googled how much yoga teachers made. The numbers were surprising. I had falsely assumed they earned next to nothing and often worked for free, but that wasn't the case.

That night I showed my mother the results of my search and gave her a blueprint of what I thought my next move should be, thinking it would change her mind. It didn't. My father, on the other hand, was very supportive of the idea. Looking back, this wasn't all that surprising; he and I had a great relationship.

Within a month I had saved up enough money to purchase my first yoga training through Yogafit. Yogafit was my saving grace. I met like-minded individuals who shared the same passion, and it was a safe space to express excitement about our similar journeys. At first it was uncomfortable opening up and being around so much love because it wasn't something expressed in my home.

For the next two years I diligently followed my blueprint, both in and out of the yoga studio. I continued to travel from training to training until I reached the required two hundred hours to receive my certificate. At the same time I did whatever I could to educate myself on building the life that I wanted. The book *Creative Visualization by Shakti Gawain*, which was required reading for one of my yoga teacher trainings, was instrumental for me, particularly because of the transformative activities at the end of each chapter.

I created vision boards and affirmation cards of my ideal life, as well as a sacred space in my loft where I devoted my mornings and evenings to this daily practice. I would read each affirmation card and then chant the affirmation five times. My personal mantra was "Everything I want comes easily and effortlessly to me."

YouTube was also an excellent resource, and one I still use to this day. When I watched a useful video I would figure out how to incorporate the advice into my lifestyle. For example, several videos explained why it is imperative to have multiple sources of income, and so to bring in extra money I worked at gyms and senior homes.

No matter what I was doing, my dreams and intentions for the future were never far from my thoughts. I kept a journal in my Home Depot apron so I could jot down thoughts I wanted to manifest as they came to me. I got very specific about what I wanted and what

I needed in order to get my life where I envisioned it to be. I also started to retrain my brain to think of my aspirations in the present tense, for example, "I want or will have a yoga studio" became "I have a yoga studio." I journaled what my studio needed, including a supplies list, the staff required and the type of classes and workshops I offered. I even wrote in detail about the promotions I gave my staff for going above and beyond. I believed mentally and emotionally and in time this too would soon manifest in the physical.

One day, while sitting in the garden hut at work, I wrote five goals I really wanted to achieve on the back of a receipt and prayed on it by tapping the receipt. Looking back, I realized I was doing a form of Reiki even before I was trained on how to work with energy! I tucked the receipt into my apron and at least once a shift I would pull it out and reread my goals, both silently and aloud. I wanted them to be embedded in my subconscious so that I would never lose sight of what I really wanted.

That same year, 2017, I discovered what passive income was. For a while (and because I had a not-so-great boss) I had been infatuated with the idea of achieving financial stability without having to go to a job. I knew it was possible, because the YouTubers I had been supporting were doing it. That's all I wanted, the opportunity to live a life of freedom without being dependent upon a traditional job for income. I had to keep practicing my affirmations but I also had to take action. I began reading everything I could in order to become an expert in making passive income. (Mind you, I had no idea how I would make this work. At the time I was struggling financially and driving a 2003 Volkswagen Beetle convertible that was always breaking down!)

There was a lot of information out there, much of it confusing at first. Many of the YouTube videos I watched were about buying stock and real estate, or even tricking people into paying you! So I continued watching and reading and began to put together information on how to attract passive income, realistically and with integrity. I then shared information on a blog post, which I posted to my website, Ashleecrazyyoga.com. The blog was about creating content, YouTube videos, music, and your own merchandise, with a focus on things you could easily do from home and without buying expensive equipment. This was something my husband and I could speak to from experience. I was excited about it, but when I shared my blog post with my co-workers they thought it was silly.

"It's not a stable source of income," they said.

I knew their comments were coming from a particular perspective: they had been working at Home Depot for fifteen or more years and thought stability came only from having a full-time job. I had tried but being controlled with a schedule that came out every two weeks just wasn't for me. It was very hard to take off work and I missed a lot of family gatherings and holidays. The final straw came when my boss scheduled me for a ten-day stretch. I began searching for more yoga opportunities, and at one point was holding down my regular job and teaching fifteen to seventeen regular yoga classes a week! Grueling as it was, I stuck with it and within a year and a half I was able to leave my job and become a full time yoga instructor. That was in 2018 and I've never looked back.

I zeroed in on my business full throttle and taught my heart out in every class. One day after my Yoga Lite class at my old gym, a student said to me, "Great class, Ashlee. You are going to go very far in life. This is only the beginning." To me this was a sign to keep going no matter how tough things got. I discovered a yoga instructor on YouTube that broke down the business of yoga and how to work smarter rather than harder. To up my income, I started holding more workshops and more private classes and I taught free classes in the park for exposure. I was tired of renting out expensive rooms and never breaking even. I needed a space that was free to bring my clients to. Eventually my husband Kary and I moved into a loft that had an open space on the second floor. We called it "The Gallery" and used it to hold workshops and private yoga classes.

In 2018 I stumbled across Reiki, and though I didn't know anything about it, something called to me to sign up for one training. I loved it, and after several more trainings and certifications, I became a Reiki Master in the Usui style and have since added this modality to my healing practices. I was then able to start hosting teacher trainings for other Reiki practitioners, which is the best way to earn money for the time you've invested. People began to seek me out for this service as it is not widely offered in my area. I was so elated to be able to serve people and witness the emotional and mental break-throughs they experienced.

There is power in these hands, I thought.

I began to get the feeling that I was very close to opening my own studio. I was also starting to get a clearer vision of what that studio would look like. Over the past few years I had taught at various facilities but I never saw a community that included everyone. Where were the kid's classes? Where were the classes for those in wheelchairs? I decided I would create a studio that welcomed people of all ages and walks of life, and that this would set us apart from the others.

Last year I presented my concept at a church one of my students connected me with. They were receptive, and soon Kary and I were hosting Kids' Yoga Boot Camp classes after school. They were both educational and fun and the number of attendees quickly grew. Parents enjoyed seeing their kids happy and engaging with other children.

Then Amanda, a good friend and fellow yogi, connected me with a gym. Though I had taught yoga in gyms for years, I never used the workout machines or stepped into a weightlifting room. Now short on cash and still riding the unpredictable wave of being a yoga teacher, I was more inclined to try something outside my comfort zone, this time as a personal trainer and boot camp instructor. I had an exceptional mentor who walked me through the basics until I was comfortable teaching my own classes. It was fun but eventually I discovered why Amanda had left and that his kindness was not genuine. The underlying goal was to exploit me as a boot camp instructor to get more members to spend money at the gym. After one year I moved on.

In 2019 I created "Yoga at Bradford Beach," a free event for people to come do yoga with me and Amanda. Just the year before, I had created a similar event but no one showed up. This time, in less than a month we had over twenty thousand views! We had an amazing turn-out as well and people began to ask where I taught yoga. The Universe was truly working its magic. My classes at The Gallery were much more crowded after that!

One evening I stumbled onto a Craigslist listing for studio space for rent. It was perfect timing. All of my sources of income were pretty consistent by then and the space was in my price range. Two days later Kary and I toured the facility and it was a done deal. I signed paperwork and that same night created an event for our Grand Opening. Once again, it garnered attention and folks started to comment with interest. Imagine my shock when one day as I was leaving the gym I received a phone call from a reporter for the Journal Sentinel. She wanted to do an interview with me about my grand opening!

Today, I am the proud and very happy owner of my own studio, Ashlee's Crazy Yoga. It took years of hard work, both physical and spiritual, but it is everything I dreamed of, for myself and the diverse community I serve. I often look back on the journal I created while working at Home Depot in 2017 and am always amazed to see all that has come to fruition. I've learned many lessons along my transformative journey, and I can sum them up like this; things don't happen overnight, but when you take yourself off autopilot and take control of your life, you can and will manifest your wildest dreams.

ABOUT THE AUTHOR: Ashlee Tuck is a Vinyasa yoga instructor, Sound Therapist, Reiki educator, Somatic Therapist, personal trainer, and owner of Ashlee's Crazy Yoga. Ashlee, who has been teaching yoga for over five years and practicing for six is passionate about making wellness accessible for everyone, regardless of age and life-style. Creating Ashlee's Crazy Yoga has given her the opportunity to bring yoga to communities and uncommon venues such as churches, senior homes, and beaches. Ashlee currently resides in Oak Creek, Wisconsin with her husband Kary.

Ashlee Tuck
Ashlee's Crazy Yoga
Ashleecrazyyoga.com
Ashleecrazyyoga@gmail.com
414-403-8227

Cocoons & Butterflies
Cindy Lybbert

"If nothing ever changed, there'd be no butterflies."
~Anonymous

I was six years old when my father bought the farm—ten acres of land with a three- bedroom house for my parents, five sisters, my brother and me. It would have been even more crowded, but my two oldest sisters had already moved out. During weekdays in the summer, my father would head out to work while the rest of us worked the farm, feeding the animals, picking fruit, and changing sprinklers, to name a few of the things we did. It was extremely hard work and the long hot days seemed to drag on forever. Though I was grateful for the fresh delicious fruit, room to run around barefoot, working beside my mother and sisters, and the cool nights when I threw a blanket down in the backyard and slept under the billions of tiny stars, I couldn't wait for school to begin.

My excitement soon turned to hate, mostly because of the bullying that went on there. The first bully I encountered was my first-grade teacher. She would call me up in front of the class and slap my palms with a wooden ruler because I pronounced my R's wrong. She would also regularly accuse me of talking and put tape across my mouth and send me out in the hall. I would stand there, completely humiliated and waiting for the bell to ring so I could dash into the bathroom and peel off the tape before anyone could see me.

I learned early on I couldn't trust the adults in my life, and never told them what was going on at school. I also stayed away from my father, who was very verbally abusive. Instead, I started building a cocoon around myself for protection. Little did I know the effects of this abuse would stay with me even through my adult years. I became quiet and shy, afraid to been seen or heard.

Good days came, when it rained I didn't have to work so hard or when the work was all finished early. Often, I'd be sitting on the cool grass or the porch just resting until I spotted a caterpillar. It made my whole day. I was mesmerized by the little caterpillar and gently pick it up, allow it to crawl on my hands and arms and stroke its soft back. I was in awe that such a funny little creature could lose all those tiny legs, do whatever it does in a cocoon, grow wings, and fly away.

Oh I wanted to be that butterfly!…Free, seen, loved and beautiful. Free to fly from my childhood nightmare. Whenever I saw a butterfly I'd stop what I was doing and just watch it until it was out of my sight. Again, I was in awe to see their transformation with their delicate, beautiful, colorful wings.

Once I was with my younger sister when a butterfly landed on me. "Do you know what it means when a butterfly lands on you?" she asked. I said no. "It's a sign of new beginnings and liberation." That gave me great comfort.

A butterfly represents patience, courage, and transformation during tough times. It's reminding you that better times are ahead.

I first heard God's voice when I was just seven years old. I was sitting in a large recliner in the living room, where I had gone to sneak a moment of escape from the summer work. I was feeling…empty and sad. The voice wasn't loud or scary, but calming and loving. And though I had never heard it before, I knew I wasn't imagining things. There was no one else in the room and besides, no one in my life spoke to me like that.

Sixty-three years later I still remember the feelings of comfort and love and "This too shall pass." I can still remember how God was there when I needed Him. This experience gave me hope and comfort throughout the years, as did PSALMS 23, which I was encouraged to memorize.

The Lord is my shepherd; I shall not want.
He maketh me to lie down in green pastures: he leadeth me
beside the still waters.
He restoreth my soul: he leadeth me in the paths of righteous-
ness for his name's sake.
Yea, though I walk through the valley of the shadow of death,
I will fear no evil: for thou Art with me: thy rod and thy staff
they comfort me.
Thou prepares a table before me in the presence of mine en-
emies: thou anointest my head with oil; my cup runneth over.
Surely goodness and mercy shall follow me all the days of my
life: and I will dwell in the house of the Lord for-ever.

Eventually, I put myself through college and received my Associate degree in Graphics & Commercial Art. I enjoyed college and started to make friends and date. At twenty-six I got married, thinking I had found my partner for life, but after ten years together my husband wanted a divorce. This triggered feelings of: rejection, abandonment, disappointment, regret, fear, and depression. There was also the responsibility of providing for my two little children on my own. The child support wasn't enough and before I knew it I was homeless and living off the government. It was only with the help of my sisters that I was able to get back on my feet, find a job, and move into a two-bedroom apartment.

I also noticed my children were experiencing the same confusion, hurt, anger, and sorrow I was. It broke my heart and there were days I wanted to crawl under a rock and die. And if it wasn't for my miracle babies, I might have done just that.

When my children became young teens, I started going through a phase of having anger and crying spells. I had no idea what was going on. Then one day I heard God's voice once again: *"It's time to heal."* I had no idea what that meant, but shortly thereafter the days became so unbearable I turned to Him for help, direction, and strength. I was hardly eating and sleeping. One day a friend suggested I see a counselor to deal with the painful memories, many of which I had dissociated from, that had started flooding back with scary regularity.

Like many who have gone through trauma, I had a hard time articulating my feelings. Fortunately I was blessed with the ability to write them. I started journaling and putting my feelings into poetry. It was a blessing and the first step toward healing.

I also found inspiring books to read—Helen Keller's biography, *The Power of Positive Thinking* by Norman Vincent Peale, and the King James Version Bible. I would simply open the book and find before me the scripture I needed. Other days I was encouraged to open certain books or I'd be in the bookstore and one would catch my eye, as if it had jumped out just for me.

At age forty-five I learned what an 'Inner Child' was and listened to mine explain to me what had happened. Each day I turned to God for strength, comfort, and healing. Sometimes, when I needed to release the frustration, fear, and pent-up feelings, I would scream in my pillow, go jogging, or soak in salt baths and listen to music.

After six months of counseling I knew there was nothing more the therapist could do for me. I *felt* I needed to heal on a deeper level… heal from the inside out! Then a friend showed me a flyer for: The Academy of Healing Arts. It was exactly what I had been looking for. I had been having health issues and my doctors couldn't, or wouldn't, do anything for me. I didn't have health insurance back then, so they'd usually just send me home with a prescription for depression.

I started taking classes at The Academy, where I learned Reiki, therapeutic touch, energy exchange, mindfulness meditation, centering, chakras, basic facts of essential oils, reflexology, kinesiology, and massage. I started to heal from the inside out and it felt wonderful…free-ing.

Over the years I also learned the meaning of abuse on all levels: verbal/emotional, physical, sexual, mental/psychological, spiritual, cultural/identity, and even financial/economic abuse and narcissism.

They carry deep and lasting wounds that need to be healed in order for one to become whole. Sometimes there is still work to be done even after the wounds are healed. My long list included being seen and heard, feeling safe, releasing fear, speaking in public, speaking my truths, saying no when I meant no and yes when I meant yes, overcoming shyness, taking care of myself, stop multi-tasking and being a perfectionist, learn to laugh, love, enjoy life, trust, and stand up for myself. I remind myself there is never any going back to what was, only moving FORWARD! We are Spiritual Beings having a human experience and we should never "should" on ourselves.

I went through another painful period of adjustment when my children left home. Caring for them had been my priority for so long that without them I felt I had no purpose. On the other hand there were several good things on the horizon. I remarried, this time to a good man who supported me in my healing journey and in starting my own business. I overcame health issues, including depression, PTSD, and hypoglycemia, and discovered new meaning to my life as I continued to learn the healing arts.

I always felt divinely guided to certain healing modalities and after I became certified I once again heard His voice: *Now take it to the world.*

I literally laughed out loud! I wasn't trying to be disrespectful, but…me?! The one who had grown up so shy and quiet, *NO thank you*! Here I was, arguing with Spirit, when I heard His voice say (with love and compassion), *And you think you are the only one deserving of healing?* Well, I couldn't argue with that!—I told God I would do it, but He would have to show me how and give me the strength.

I also made a decision to no longer wallow in drama, trauma, fear, or pain. As tempting as it was to stay in my own cocoon, I learned ignoring my past, the healing, and the truth was a surefire way to remain stuck in that awful, doomed feeling of hurt and despair. Suddenly, the words *"…and the truth shall make you free"* had a whole new, wonderful meaning to it.

Allowing myself to spread my wings and fly has brought me to a place where I can now serve others around the world, helping them to heal their wounds and create miracles. And what a blessing it has been for me to see happiness and life come back into men, women, and children.

I hope others find joy, purpose, and healing now and forever. There's only one thing we can take with us when we leave this life, and that's what we have learned and what we have done to make things better for ourselves and others.

Make a commitment now to change your mind, and you will indeed change your life. Through my transformation I learned:

- God hears us and is always there to support us in our healing journey.
- Self approval and self-acceptance are the keys to positive changes.
- Good health begins by loving ourselves.
- If we spend our whole lives worrying we will never know happiness.
- There's great strength and courage in overcoming trauma.
- To ask not "Why did this happen to me?" but "How can I transform this into something better?"
- "To accept the things we cannot change, to have the courage to change the things we can, and the wisdom to know the difference." ~Serenity Prayer
- Work, play, sleep, wholesome activities, and healthy eating are crucial to a balanced life, health, and happiness.
- Forgiveness is the key to happiness, peace of mind, and healing.
- Forgiveness comes in the right time, we cannot force it. Forgiving others helps us to heal fully. We leave the rest and the judgment to God, so we no longer have to carry that burden.
- The only difference between the words journey and journal

are the last two letters!

- Healing does not have to be alone, scary, hard, difficult, or hell. God shows us what we need to know and He can do that in many different ways.
- And finally, *...arise with healing in [your] wings. And you will go free, leaping with joy.* *~Malachi 4:2*

Healing is possible.

ABOUT THE AUTHOR: Cindy Fay Lybbert is a testament to the power of faith and the courage of Spirit. Through courageous perseverance and keen desire to thrive, she overcame life challenges and discovered a Divine calling to be of service to others. As an Empath and Master in the Healing Arts, Cindy takes clients on a "healing journey" that helps transform their wounds and create miracles. She takes great joy in helping men, women, and children around the world heal on all levels of abuse, healing Mind, Body and Spirit. She knows that healing can happen quickly and easily; she also believes in the power of faith and that God is the ultimate Healer.

Cindy Fay Lybbert
Master Intuitive Energy Healer
fullhealingjourney.com
cindyfay02@gmail.com
503-757-2508

Resilience in Adversity
Taeko McNish

My name is Taeko and I am originally from Tokyo, Japan. I am the mother of two grown children and, after years of training, education, and commitment, the owner of a business committed to instilling confidence in women with well-deserved attention and personalized treatment. I used to live a very different life. however; I was a housewife—an experience which brought me comfort and joy. Everything changed dramatically when I lost the structure of my life as I knew it—I became single, moved far from my family, and could no longer satisfy my routine habits of compassion and care.

These dramatic changes marked the beginning of a years-long transformation accompanied by fear, roadblocks, and the unexpected. It is my hope that in sharing my journey and the places it took me I will inspire you to believe that anyone, including you, can adopt new beliefs to fuel a healthy and joy-filled life.

When I introduce myself, people ask me, "What does Taeko mean?" The answer to this question lies in my religious upbringing, one grounded in Buddhist beliefs and open to the guidance of oracles and their prophecies. My name is derived from a Buddhist chant that symbolizes the strangeness, mysticism, and wonder in life. Growing up it was just my mother and me, and though it was sometimes lonely having such a small family in a city as large as Tokyo I was grateful that she raised me to live as I pleased, free to choose any path. That path would take me overseas to the United States and married to a man from the Midwest. A few years later, I also had two gifted children who gave me energy and spiced up my joyful life.

Knowing I was a role model for my children, I constantly strived to improve myself and became educated so they would be inspired to do the same. I started by obtaining a GED, then degrees from various colleges and universities while learning English along the way. Taking classes and raising my children was no easy task, and my own self-care often fell by the wayside, but the reward—doing something good for myself and my family—was well worth the challenges. Everything was going so well, right up until the moment my husband announced that he had decided to leave our relationship.

The news completely blindsided me. In Japan, a high priority is placed on keeping families together, and divorce is very rare. For me, it felt like the end of the world—the structure of my life was collapsing and my identity as a housewife was shifting. After a year of fighting the divorce, I realized how unhealthy this was. I had to shift my point of view from feeling victimized to feeling empowered.

I thought I would heal with time, and when this didn't happen, I sought professional help from a counselor. Having someone to speak with in a safe environment gave me the validation I needed to be able to move forward. It changed my perspective in ways I could not have done on my own. Something I practiced quite a bit during that time, and still do, is positive self-talk. This enabled me to become my own validator, confident in my resilience and desires. I was nearly fifty years old, and about to undergo an enormous transformation.

Healing and uncovering my passions stood hand-in-hand. I began opening up to myself and becoming curious about my values. I had always felt a large capacity to care, something I tapped into daily as a mother. I also was motivated by a continuous desire to learn, as evidenced from the degrees I had pursued, including one in Biology. I started to wonder, what if I explored the intersection between caring and health and wellness? I continued my education, becoming a Nursing Assistant, an aesthetician, and a massage therapist, and in doing so discovered my passions for informing and providing health services to women and elderly people.

As I began to feel more like myself, I was able to spend more time considering my priorities and what I wanted to get out of this life. I also realized that if I wanted to be helpful to others, I would first need to become an expert at caring for myself. In the meantime, I was already putting my newfound skills to use, helping to bring healing to the world around me while building confidence in my abilities. Then I was dealt another curveball: the spa where I worked was closing its doors…the next day! It was the push I needed to step out in faith and open my own wellness spa.

Running Taeko Aesthetics LLC has given me a sense of contentment and joy I never experienced before. Not only am I able to put my passion to work when meeting with my clients, I also enjoy the process of preparing for sessions and watching my business grow. Everything I learned over the years, both educationally and through life experiences, has prepared me to be where I am today. While challenging, losing the structure in my life all those years ago has led me down a path I would never have thought possible. It freed me to pursue my goals and further my education; it also pushed me to take chances that helped me grow and, ultimately, know what it feels like to be happy in my own skin.

At times we can feel boxed in by circumstances, like there is no way out, no chance for things to change, and no chance for happiness in the future. While such times are grueling and feel impossible to move through, there is always a moment of malleability from which you can start something new. Reaching out to a professional at this moment is crucial. Having another perspective, especially someone who is certified, can give you professional validation for you and the life you live.

When my family structure fell apart, the expectations for my life did as well. I felt I would never be on equal footing again. This, I now know, was the beginning of my transformative process. Over the years I have learned to roll with the punches. Now, when something out of my control occurs, I don't panic; I let it take me to a new place. Even if it feels like I am reaching a dead end, I accept the changes and see the different paths I can travel. I see everything as an opportunity to adapt and grow.

I also learned to make my self-care a top priority. My job requires me to be a role model for others. I am the person my clients come to for healing and therefore I must nourish myself each day so I can be prepared to share with them. I meditate and exercise daily, eat well, and take time to learn. Knowing that I can provide care in a person's life keeps me motivated to be as healthy as I can be. I've come to a place in which I feel called to come out of my comfort zone and share my story to help others. I would like to share how a positive mindset, listening to your body, setting boundaries, and behavior change has helped me live healthier and stay resilient in the face of stress and fear.

A positive mindset keeps me focused on what I love about life when stress and challenges arise. I remind myself that when one door closes, another one opens. For example, getting fired from a job is a painful experience, and pain is a signal of change. When you maintain a positive attitude, you remember that there will be a place that better suits your passions or leads you to a more fulfilling purpose in life. Whatever that experience may have been, you have a capacity to grow beyond it and step into something newer and better. When you are willing to open your mind, ideas will come to you and release you from your captor.

The practice of listening to my body gives me insight into eating healthy—something everyone needs to set themselves up for physiological success. With so much information out there on this topic, it can easily become overwhelming and prevent you from acting. Rather than following methods of eating like vegetarianism, veganism, or keto, I listen to what my stomach and brain ask me for: plenty of fresh vegetables and fish. I also found that I feel stronger when I keep processed foods and wheat products to a minimum. When feeling stuck, I remember to think positively and listen to what my body is asking for, be it diet, exercise, or rest.

Setting healthy boundaries has helped me gain control of my life and see the true benefits of good communications. Speaking up for myself is one way to ensure those boundaries are respected. I used to believe that keeping my negative feelings hidden was an act of kindness, that I was protecting someone from my negativity. What I learned, however, is that this often leads to miscommunication and conflict. I've learned that being open about your feelings can bring you closer to others. Again, working with a professional can, in my opinion, be vital to setting boundaries and regaining control of your life. A health coach, for example, can help you uncover the person you want to become; create a roadmap to get there, and hold you accountable along the way. They guide you through behavioral changes as you learn to stay positive, listening to your body, and set boundaries.

Changing your behavior can be difficult, especially when you do it on your own and/or when you're surrounded by people practicing unhealthy norms. In fact, many people feel like they must conform to these norms in order to fit in, or that they might lose the people most important to them if they act differently. This fear will keep you from changing, however, and the happiness you're hoping for will not come unless action is taken. There are always ways to engage with the ones you love while also putting yourself in a better situation for success. I found that if you make a small change in one area of life, another will change too. This means that you have the power to create your own life and craft it to your will, and making a better choice each time the opportunity is presented will reveal to you the life you were meant to live.

I would like to end my story with gratitude to all the teachers who have helped me expand my awareness, and to other like-minded people in my life who have let me know that I'm a part of everyone and loved and protected by the Universe. I am also very thankful for the difficult situations I've experienced in my life, for this adversity pushed me to learn, try new things, and grow. It took me fifty years to get to where I am now, but it does not have to be this way. Any time is a good time to begin. You also don't have to wait for life to go downhill or experience more pain to take a step forward. Now is the perfect time to transform, and the first step is for you to take care of yourself!

ABOUT THE AUTHOR: Taeko McNish is a health and wellness coach who strives to help clients navigate the complexities of their lives and discover their potential. Taeko holds a degree in Biology and is a certified aesthetician, massage therapist, and Reiki master. At her wellness spa, Taeko Aesthetics LLC, she puts her knowledge to practice with medical aesthetics, therapeutic massage therapy, Reiki sessions, and wellness coaching. She recently completed extensive training through the Health Coach Institute and the Mayo Clinic Wellness coach training program. Taeko also utilizes Motivational Interviewing and Neuro-Linguistic techniques to enable clients to achieve better health and quality of life.

Taeko McNish
Taeko Aesthetics LLC
taeko.skincaretherapy.net
taekoremedy@gmail.com
608-492-0022

Daring to Risk
Sandy Levey-Lunden

I haven't changed much since I was seven years old, when I started pestering my mother with questions like, "Why are you here? What are you here for?" Occasionally I would even ask, "Why did God send you?" A single thought constantly repeated in my mind: *What is our real purpose?* I didn't even know what that word meant, but knew I needed an answer.

My mother was completely shocked that such a young person was asking her such deep, thought-provoking questions. She tried her best to find answers that would satisfy me but they never did. One day she proudly announced, "I'm here to be your mother!" To that I responded, "If you're really here to be my mother, if that is your real purpose, then you would be happy!" You see, I had noticed much of the time that she appeared to be quite unhappy. She also suffered from painful migraine headaches and nausea that left her helpless in bed for days at a time. She didn't seem to be passionate about her life; she wasn't smiling, laughing, or enthusiastic. I felt that if she was enjoying her life, she would have had more exuberance.

Clearly the seeds of my becoming a life coach and counselor were planted very early on, maybe even before I was born. My grandmother, Gussie, had great abilities to heal people. She was my guide and mentor always. She was selfless and entirely giving. I don't think I ever heard her say no to anyone. In turn, I have always tried to find a way to say yes as well. I believe that if someone has been attracted to ask me something, there must be some purpose in it for me, something I'm supposed to say yes to.

We all have a destiny in the way we move through our lives. In looking backwards from the present to the past, we can see what has shaped that destiny, flow, and meaning in our lives. I was always looking for the highest use of myself—where I would be the most helpful and have the greatest effect, given my talents, abilities, and natural gifts.

In many ways, I didn't have a childhood at all; I had an exploration of giant questions: What is the meaning of life? What are we here for? Who can I assist, and in what way? Many years later I found this saying in *A Course in Miracles:* "I am here to be only truly helpful." This simple quote embodies exactly how I feel, think, and live.

In 1979, I was a career counselor working with migrant workers for the Monterey Office of Education in Salinas, California. Although it was meaningful work, I felt I could do so much more with my life. In 1980, for the very first time, I decided to go head-first with my fear of success. I had read a description of a three-day women's workshop, Women's Success Team (WST), which had been created by coach, author, and thought-leader Barbara Sher and was now being hosted by a woman named Laura Boxer. It completely resonated with me, and before I knew it, I was participating alongside other women in the first WST seminar on the West Coast.

My experience in the WST was incredibly emotional; I cried throughout the entire course, more than anybody else in the room. I felt like I had made a tremendous breakthrough, like I was able to feel my blocks and finally release them.

I had also thoroughly enjoyed the process—the introspective examining, thinking, feeling, and sharing with the other women. I had never before seen the power of such a support network and was so excited at the prospect of what we could accomplish together.

Upon completion of the course, we were grouped into teams who would continue to offer each other support. We didn't all live near each other, but we could talk on the phone and we sometimes met in person. I was fully inspired by this new adventure with these wonderful women.

To my great surprise, Laura Boxer asked me to be the Director of Marketing for the West Coast WST. I didn't even know what marketing was at that time and had to look it up in the dictionary! It said marketing is the way something is put out into the world for people to buy, see, and have. Laura kept calling me and asking me to move to San Francisco and help her find a house for the WST course, where we both would live and hold the seminars. I was amazed that she kept asking me. I really thought she should find someone else, but Laura didn't agree. On some level she knew I was the one to help her, and that others could avail themselves of my support as well.

There is a characteristic inside me that I discovered over many years of living: I would always rise to the occasion. I would always find a way to get it done, whatever it was, and accomplish the task at hand. Even when I wanted to give up, there was a part of me that would always keep going. So, despite my trepidations, I gave notice at my job and headed for the Bay Area. When I arrived, Laura informed me that we didn't have all the money we needed to rent a house. We would have to produce a seminar to raise the funds… and we only had a week to do it!

Anxiety, worry, and fear consumed my thoughts, so much so that I usually slept only three hours a night during this period. Miraculously, I came up with a way to market the WST course. I knew if I could address a group of women every single evening, I could enroll enough to hold a seminar each weekend. We would then have enough money to complete the payment for the house and other expenses. With no time to waste, I immediately put my plan into action—speaking to women each night, then following up with them on the phone the next day. The conversations felt natural, as I had a personal connection with everyone I spoke with. This was because my interest was very genuine; always coming from my heart and a sense of purposefulness. It was like I was growing everyone I enrolled in WST into a powerful, successful woman. This was during the Women's Movement, and many of the women I was meeting were recently divorced and on their own for the first time in their lives. When someone was afraid, I was right there supporting her to work through the fear. I said, "Do whatever it is you are afraid to do. That's how you make a fear disappear."

Every night, with a map in my hand, I ventured to a different part of the San Francisco Bay area to connect to someone who had a group of women either at their home, office, organization, or library. I would then deliver a speech to acquaint them with the WST program. Back then, there were very few seminars of this intimate and personal nature where one could get this kind of support and guidance to create a vision for a life they dreamed of, using their natural talents and innate abilities. Even without formal training, we could directly teach ourselves what we wanted to learn. The WST always filled in with ideas, contacts, methods, referrals, and concrete support. It was a pooled and beautiful effort. Participants would loan each other their clothes, their bookbags, their homes; whatever it took to help each other succeed.

We generated a level of enthusiasm and passion I had never seen before. It was palpable, so much so that I could enroll pretty much anyone I spoke to in the WST. I was very successful at marketing this course, through sheer will and a determination to keep learning and growing. With everything I faced a learning curve because I was doing it for the first time, and at the same time I was finding the method inside me. I learned to be a public speaker and spoke only from the heart. I even appeared on national television! I thought this experience would be terrifying, but I ended up loving it.

And so it was that in taking one of the biggest risks of my life I found one of my greatest abilities: helping women achieve their dreams. Each weekend, I made new friends and supporters who went on to attend other courses and refer others to WST. There were very few weekends that we didn't hold a WST course, and each was a unique three-day adventure that sometimes lasted late into the night. At the end of each course, I felt so fulfilled. I was living my life on purpose.

Another miracle occurred when I put out a newspaper ad to sell my rare, vintage Mercedes convertible. A man named Justin Sterling replied to the ad and I knew intuitively that our meeting would have a profound implication in my life.

As Justin drove my red Mercedes throughout San Francisco, we had provocative discussions, mainly about women, sex, and power. It was all aligned with what I was working on with the Women's Success Team. Justin seemed to love to talk to women, think about them, and empower them. I told him I could enroll a course called Women, Sex & Power and he could write the content and teach the course. He loved the idea and we began working on it shortly thereafter.

There were seventy-five women in attendance at the first Women, Sex & Power course. Justin was extremely daring in his delivery, which increased my fear that I would be judged. I had done a daring thing in helping him create Women, Sex & Power and now I was worried the women wouldn't agree with the content, and about how my friends would view me. It was a very scary time, for in my mind there was a lot at stake; sometimes I could hardly breathe because of my fear and anxiety. During the first course, Justin wouldn't even allow me in the room. My fears were definitely confirmed when the women expressed shock by how boldly Justin presented himself and men and women in relationship. Fortunately, I didn't lose any friends or supporters over it.

It didn't take much to convince Justin to cultivate the men's market. We named the men's course Men, Sex & Power, or "The Gorilla Training." Over the next two months I enrolled one hundred and seventy-five men. At one point in the course the men would begin to act out their gorilla nature until it became an energetic free-for-all of male "macho-ness." Justin wanted every man to access power in their male nature which, he believed, turned women on. It was extreme, and quite frightening for me to be the only woman in the room during this time.

About one year after our initial meeting, Justin and I had a difference of opinion regarding his philosophy. He believed men got all their power from women and were completely lost on their own. He also felt that women were in charge of every relationship, and if it didn't work out it was the woman's fault. I didn't agree with these concepts. I knew I had to leave and go on a different journey to find out how I could represent this connection between men and women. In 1995, I created a course called True Woman's Power and I have presented this course continuously ever since.

It was extremely challenging to leave Justin and the seminar we had created together, and I would spend many years questioning whether or not I had made the right decision. Looking back, though, I know I followed my heart and that is always the right thing to do.

Contrary to Justin's philosophy, I saw men and women as a circle, supporting each other continuously with no end and no beginning. This never-ending circle is extremely powerful when there is a unified purpose and passion for this purpose. Today I call this connection a Holy Relationship. In this relationship, each person sees the other as a Divine, unlimited being. Their function together is to support each other and see each other as eternally innocent, no matter what they might think of themselves or each other.

As I continued my work around our relationships with ourselves and with each other, I realized that guilt was the root of much of the conflict; it created blocks that prevented people from moving forward. In 1990, through prayer I was given the Power of Clearing Process, a unique and powerful method of releasing mental and emotional blocks. Over the years, I have used this process to clear thousands of people from their perceived guilt and help them to live "on purpose" with who they *truly* are.

I would say that 1980 and 1981 were the most exciting years of my life. Everything that I was doing in my career was new to me; almost every day presented some new task I had never undertaken before. I had to find the answers deep within myself as to how to market these two seminar businesses and create a support system for the women to continue their learning. Both seminars, WST and Women, Sex & Power, had graduate support teams to keep the learning alive and the women moving forward in their evolving process of success and relationship.

Looking back, the reason that first WST course resonated so deeply with me was that it was aligned with my lifelong curiosity about *why we are here*. At the same time, it was the beginning of a decades-long transformative process that allowed me to shift limiting beliefs and face down my fears. Of all my many discoveries along this journey, one thing stands out: everything is about courage—the courage to be your True self and decide that your journey to be at peace, love and Oneness is the ultimate purpose of your life.

ABOUT THE AUTHOR: Sandy Levey-Lunden is an international speaker, counselor, and life coach of over forty years. She has created twenty-four original seminars, each in response to a challenge presented to her by someone during one of their life coaching or counseling sessions. Sandy was one of the first and original life coaches in the 1980s, before such a career even existed. Her unique style of coaching has helped over 40,000 people in North America, Australia, and Europe to heal their past negative beliefs, traumas, personal pain, and relationship challenges. Sandy lived in Sweden for eleven years and now resides in beautiful Bellingham, Washington in the Pacific Northwest.

Sandra Levey-Lunden
On Purpose
sandylevey.com
onpurpose@sandylevey.com
360-527-2796

Disguised Gifts
Sarah Lascano

My first awareness, aside from the alarm interrupting my fitful sleep, was of oppressive nausea. My hand fumbled around on the nightstand, trying to find a cracker without having to sit up or move my head. My only thought was to avoid another dreaded bout of vomiting.

The rest of the day was much the same, the term "morning sickness" clearly a misnomer. I ate as slowly as possible, feeling at any moment I might lose the battle of keeping food down. While driving, my eyes constantly searched for places I could pull over if I suddenly had to vomit. Four months into my first pregnancy, I moved through my days in a haze of misery, resentful that this supposedly joyous time was so horrible for me.

I was still feeling queasy that night as I sat across from my husband in a local eatery and searched the menu for something that wouldn't send my stomach into full revolt. Little did I know that a three-day food poisoning event was about to unfold, forever transforming my gut health, immune system, digestion, and nervous system. It was to be the beginning of a fifteen-year health and spiritual discovery journey.

I grew up in a loving, achievement-oriented family, blessed with ample resources for experiencing the world. There was lots of work and play, much of it fueled by stress. Competitive swimming dominated my early years. Double workouts and hard physical exercise left little time for sleep. I placed high expectations upon myself and developed performance anxiety at swim meets. In high school, I taught a religious school class and worked in the local hospital as a nursing assistant and ward secretary, as well as an office assistant and surgery assistant in my father's surgical practice. I learned a tremendous amount about people, the world, the body. While in high school I also started an environmental club, was an officer in the student government, and was involved in countless other activities. On weekends, when I wasn't working outside the home, I gardened, cut wood, or helped with other home maintenance tasks. I constantly pushed my body and mind to the limit. Rest, I felt, was idle and selfish. There was so much to achieve and so little time.

This way of living gave me tremendous exposure and experience but it also strained my body. By the time I was twelve, I had reactive hypoglycemia—blood sugar dips after eating—which I now realize was a sign of significant adrenal stress. In fact, I became so overcommitted in high school that I vowed to never put myself in that position again. I succeeded in keeping that promise to myself, but new life stresses were just around the corner.

I made my way through college as many good students do: lots of studying and lots of stressing about grades. I still managed to exceed expectations, obtaining two Industrial Engineering degrees, working as a student tutor, leading an honor society, and completing work internships. After graduating I wanted to take a week or two off but found myself giving in to the pleas of my new employer, who needed me to start immediately. Once again I was focusing on achievement with no ability to set healthy boundaries for myself. The idea of restorative downtime was completely foreign to me.

My twenties found new cities, new jobs, and more unbalance, though to me the fast pace with minimal to no recovery time felt normal. My technical sales job took me on frequent one-day or overnight trips, which meant grueling hours and lack of sleep. I managed client and coworker relationships with people much more senior than myself, placing me in stress-filled situations for which I had little experience. Presenting to Fortune 500 firms and people twice my age was intimidating, though I did enjoy the thrill. I also over-exercised with power yoga, spin classes, and cardio. This helped my sleep by burning off extra cortisol, but unbeknownst to me, all the stress was continuing to weaken my body and perfectly set me up for the crash that would occur a few years later.

During this first part of my life, I believed as many of us do, that if I avoided negative emotions, I was a responsible and professional adult. If my life was under my control, I could feel I was succeeding. If events happened that I couldn't control, I had failed. I focused on achievement and approval from others to judge my worth. Stress was an inherent part of me: I had no idea how to navigate the world without it. And certainly my environment did not offer much training or coaching in this regard.

My thirties brought major life changes all within a few years: marriage, the selling and purchasing of homes, a new job and, becoming pregnant with my first child. I had the advanced degrees, a lucrative career, a lovely house, a fabulous husband. All perfect. A few months later that fateful food poisoning event provided the impetus for the glass house to start to crumble. In that moment, all control was stripped from my tightly wound life. Within two weeks, I had hip pain, joint pain, eczema, and further digestive issues. In a few months, my newborn son had colic and an amped-up nervous system from exposure to my body's stress. I felt completely overwhelmed and, for the first time in my life, couldn't see a path forward.

For my journey, this loss of control was rooted in a physical health journey and parenting struggles. For others, it could be depression, loss of a loved one, major physical injury, an identity crisis. These situations make us dig deep, force us to leave the confines of our comfortable reality, and pave the way for transformation.

Significantly sleep deprived, physically and emotionally wounded by birth trauma, and juggling digestive issues in both me and my newborn, I started my quest for answers. We bounced from one doctor to another, finally landing at a holistic medical practice. Food testing revealed my son and I were sensitive to ninety percent of the foods we were eating, but no one could tell us how to fix the problems. Rotation diets, strange bread made from only sweet potatoes, and a constant feeling of not being safe when eating became our reality. The engineer in me knew there had to be a solution, but two years later it continued to elude us and I had added full-blown chronic fatigue to my health challenges. Finally, I received a diagnosis of adrenal burnout and began searching for health providers who could help me start climbing out of this huge hole that was thirty-five years in the making.

I continued to move from practitioner to practitioner, still believing my journey was all about the physical. Eventually, the mind-body connection and energy healing started coming into my life, but it would take another big trauma to pave the way for deeper understanding.

It happened while I was pet-sitting Maggie, the truck-chasing, pint-sized yorkie my sister loved like a child. Somehow the leash didn't lock and she darted into the path of a dump truck. The shock and guilt of her death took an incredible toll on my already weakened body.

Though I didn't realize it at the time, Maggie was about to give me one of the greatest gifts of my life: the conscious feeling of energy. Her remains were in our basement freezer awaiting my sister's decisions, and we could not go down there without a tremendous feeling of unease. This was more than an emotional reaction. We realized it the moment we removed her remains and this feeling immediately vanished. One afternoon, my husband suddenly felt uneasy and called to see if I was okay. We later learned that was the exact moment Maggie was cremated. This marked a major turning point in the way I understood the world: there was far more to be acknowledged than just my five sense perceptions.

As the years rolled by, energy healing became a key part of my healing. Digestion improved, energy started to return, hormones began to balance. I began using EFT, just five minutes per day, and started to see noticeable results. I researched emotion lists, for I had no idea how to feel or label emotions within myself. I began pushing myself to tune into what I was feeling and try to recognize information that came to my awareness (for instance, dreams/memories of my childhood). I started feeling lighter, with less stress and less reactiveness with my son. With each practitioner visit, I released more emotions, belief systems, and past stresses from my body. At about the six-year mark, my second pregnancy began and with it, another new gift.

During my fourth month of pregnancy, I woke at three a.m. with my forehead buzzing. The slow rhythmical buzzing would last until I woke in the morning, only to return the next night. I feared I was sensitive to EMFs from electricity and worried if baby and I were safe. I traveled among beds and sofas in the house, looking for a place where I could escape the buzzing. I found no solution. Baby finally arrived and the buzzing stopped, only to suddenly resume three months later. This time, I was in full scientific engineer mode! I purchased blocking cloth intended for grounding and shielding while sleeping. I wrapped my entire head in this cloth, confident I would be protected from this invisible EMF situation, only to awake the next morning to the same buzzing. It suddenly dawned on me this buzzing had nothing to do with manmade energy and everything to do with spiritual/ethereal energy. Wow, this was certainly bizarre. I let this fact sink into the deepest parts of my psyche. Blessedly, all fear of the buzzing suddenly vanished and curiosity began growing like a tenacious weed. Within weeks, I woke to the feeling of circling on my palm. Fascinated, I remained still and just allowed myself to feel the sensation. I looked down, expecting to see a finger tracing circles, but nothing visible touched my hand. It felt so alive, so intriguing, so real. Approximately seven years from my initial health crash, it hit me: I was on a spiritual journey.

This realization increased my hunger for answers. We used more energy healers to release disturbances in the body and mind and we saw results. Improvements such as completely stopping food reactions were hard to deny. I realized I wanted to do this myself, to help others as our practitioners helped us. After attending classes to learn two energetic healing modalities, I was hooked.

I continued to learn more, continued to set better boundaries in my life, and decreased all sorts of stress. I learned how to create restorative downtime for myself. If relationships were draining me, I made a decision to minimize contact. I worked to understand, feel, and release emotional energy. This changed how I viewed the world. The need for control began to vanish; being more present and authentic in my daily life blossomed. At some point, I realized my current life looked nothing like it had as a young adult. I interacted with the world in a more balanced, nourishing way.

Each different technique, system, and practitioner taught me something either about myself, holistic healing, or the world. Each step loosened another layer preventing me from being myself. Sometimes, in the moment, I judged these steps as mistakes. Later I realized there are no mistakes; each step brings wisdom in one form or another. This removed the pressure of being perfect and neutralized the power of judgement (of myself and from others). I realized there is no way to judge our past actions: we are different people looking back through the lens of wisdom. I felt freedom to be authentic in each and every moment, to show up without fear of making a mistake. As I continue to travel life's experiences, some easy and some not, I realize I am indeed transformed: into greater peace, deeper authenticity and a marriage to the present moment.

ABOUT THE AUTHOR: Sarah Lascano is the founder of RayZen Energy, where she is an energy medicine and spiritual healing practitioner. She has helped hundreds of clients around the world get unstuck, find better health, gain wisdom, and transform their lives. Her popular On Demand Healing sessions are transforming the way people receive energy healing. Sarah holds engineering degrees, is an IET Master Instructor and certified BodyTalk Practitioner which she combines with knowledge of the human body to bring a powerful, grounded energy to her sessions. It is her passion to help people discover the root cause of their problems and move forward with ease and grace. She lives in western Virginia with her husband and three children.

Sarah Lascano
RayZen Energy, LLC
RayZenEnergy.com
sarah@rayzenenergy.com

Happy and Free On Purpose
Lauren G. Foster

I learned at a very young age what it means to be free and find my own way. As the youngest of six kids I was often left to my own devices while my mother was busy dealing with my five older siblings. The flip side of that freedom is that I got into some trouble that I might otherwise have been protected from: molestation, exposure to drugs and alcohol way too early, injuries and accidents, and getting beaten up by school bullies. Fortunately, I figured out pretty early that those traumas and dramas can only be the guiding force in my life if I let them. I somehow got the message that all of my experiences, good and bad, had molded me into the person I was, and I tried really hard to like that person. I could be a "victim," keeping active all of the things that had gone wrong, or I could forge ahead and try to make new choices.

I was a very religious adolescent, spending a lot of my time in church and pledging my life to missionary service when I was just thirteen. I loved the Minister of Youth and Music, as well as the creative outlet singing and acting in church plays provided me. Best of all, I felt safe and secure within the fold of a loving church family.

An unfortunate series of events would rip that safety net right out from under me. First, our youth minister went to Brazil to do missionary work. Then our pastor got caught in an indiscretion with a parishioner. As if this wasn't bad enough, a criminal set fire to the church to create a distraction so she could break her boyfriend out of jail! Just like that, my church foundation had gone up in smoke. When services resumed, the new leadership didn't resonate with me. Instead of messages of love; I now heard things like, "Be careful with your eye makeup. Your eyes are provocative and might make men think sinful thoughts." I was also supposed to give "hugs from the side," lest I make contact with my breasts and incite lust. Realizing it was no longer the church I knew and loved, my attachment to it faded away, but my love of service and my instinctual connection to God remained.

This foundation, along with the unconditional love of my family, and the lessons born of all that early freedom gave me the courage to go out and make life happen on my own terms. And I did! I am about to turn fifty-five, and at last count I've had thirty-seven jobs and moved twenty-one times. There were about sixteen relationships, including one marriage and divorce, not counting one night stands. I stopped screwing around and finally finished college; I created careers and tanked them. I did some traveling, saw some things, had a lot of fun. Yet I was always chasing happiness; never realizing that no matter where I went, I was taking my restless spirit and seeking heart with me.

I had always done well financially, well enough that I was the one my family came to for financial support. As a professional sales-person, I'd been taught to visualize successful outcomes and have high energy. I was also a student of positive psychology, the Law of Attraction, spirituality, and the power of the mind over matter. I thought I was a really good little manifester, getting things done, taking care of everybody else; full of ego and pride. So I earned and I gave. I succeeded and I fell down. I always got back up, started over, and always landed on my feet...until the day I didn't.

In 2007 I had an accidental pregnancy, and not with the right guy (I forgot to even count him in the sixteen!). But it was a happy acci-dent—I was forty-three-years old and had thought my childbearing years were behind me. Then the doctor gave me the devastating news—the fetus had not attached and I was going to miscarry. That was the beginning of my biggest downward spiral. I lost my cushy, high-paying job and decided to liquidate everything and take a sabbatical. I spent about six months in Guatemala and traveled a bit in Europe before the call of family brought me back to the States.

By that time it was late 2008 and, unbeknownst to me, the US economy had completely tanked. I bought a one-third interest in my favorite day spa, with no research, no service industry experience, no training or licensing to allow me to "work" in my own business. By 2010, I was bankrupt, jobless, and homeless, camped out in my sister's spare room. Temping at the local radio and tv stations, housesitting, and taking other odd jobs, just enough to keep me in wine and cigarettes. This was my lowest point. I had nothing, I didn't want to try to get back up, because I'd probably just have to give whatever I had to my family, or maybe I'd lose it all again.

The blows just kept coming. My brother died; my mom had to be moved to a state-run nursing home because no one had the money to pay for a better place. I had completely exhausted myself financially, emotionally, and physically with nothing to show for it. Had my sister been in a position to support me, I could have easily lived out the rest of my life just like that: aimless, purposeless, numbed by alcohol and casual sex, neither knowing nor caring what came next. But she was in an even worse place than me, and about to lose her home. As my apathy didn't extend to being on-the-streets homeless, I was forced to dig deep for the will to once again find some purpose and joy in life.

From this humble place, I realized that I wasn't anyone's hero, nor was I meant to be. Everyone has their own path and the same access to the Universe as I do; it wasn't my job to take care of them. I handed my mom, my sisters and brothers, and my beloved nephew over to God, put my blinders on and headed in the direction of what I wanted.

All those years of studying spirituality, positive psychology, and the Law of Attraction had provided me with a ton of life skills. So I pulled them all out and from the simplest of places began to rebuild my life. I didn't envision mansions and millions of dollars, fame and fortune. I created a simple dream. I wanted work that came easy to me and gave me the freedom to create my own schedule and not cap my income. I wanted a little piece of land and a small house that was very isolated. I wanted to have the freedom to have doors and windows open all the time and for my dog and cats and me to be free and safe. I wanted a place in which I could hunker down and create in solitude, serenity, silence, and peace.

Once I got clear on what I wanted and planted the vision of how that would feel in my mind, things started to happen very quickly. With one phone call I found a position as an independent contractor in advertising sales, with a product that was very reputable and pretty easy to sell. I could live anywhere and work from home. They were willing to pay a stipend to help me while I built the business. They wanted a specific end result but had no desire to dictate how I got there. I was completely free to work my way, to make my own schedule, and create my own business. It's important to note that this type of arrangement was exactly what they wanted as well, and that I had known about this opportunity for a year. I just couldn't see it because I had been assuming many things—that I would be micromanaged, that they would be demanding and make me adhere to a schedule or show up at an office. NONE of this was true and it was a perfect match.

Next, I found an area in beautiful East Tennessee, where there was a lot of the kind of property I wanted. My sister's house had finally been foreclosed on, and I was not yet in a position to purchase anything, so I found a basement apartment that I could afford and was near where I wanted to buy. It was tiny—just two hundred-fifty feet for me, my dog, and four cats—but it was nice to have my own place again. I did my work and took my dog on lots of hikes, exploring the area and looking at every property that matched my dream. I also started searching for a bank that would finance me with a brand new bankruptcy. Most importantly, I kept my eyes on the dream and my heart in the most grateful place I could find.

I made lists of positive aspects of the tiny little apartment that was my home. I praised my healthy body and my sweet pets, and my friends. Every day, I DECIDED that I would be in love with my life and that I would be excited, expectant, and have total faith that my dream home was coming, very soon.

I found a place I thought was perfect, but I could not secure financing for it yet and the owner didn't offer any other options. This troubled me NOT ONE BIT, as I knew this just meant that another, even better place was on the way. In the meantime, I stayed grateful, and I learned for myself that happiness is not something you find. Happiness is something you choose, create, and generate. I learned that when I was focused on the neighbor's loud music or my freezing apartment, I felt crappy, But when I focused on the little screened in porch with the view of the lake, or pizza delivery, or the beauty all around me, I was happy. No amount of learning and studying could measure up to what I proved to myself. You can be happy anywhere, in any situation. It just depends on where you put your attention.

One year later, I found the perfect place. It was nestled in the mountains on five acres, a fairy cottage on the outside and a log cabin on the inside. Completely open, with a high vaulted ceiling and a sweet little loft bedroom. No neighbors to speak of. Completely safe, silent, serene, and lovely. Exactly what I had envisioned; better than and half the price of the one I'd wanted and couldn't get. I still couldn't get financing, but the owner agreed to rent it to me until my bankruptcy aged one more year. And that's exactly what happened. The following year I was the owner of my dream home. I built a series of decks outside where I worked and played with my dog and cats and thrived! Long lovely hikes and picnics at lunch on my very own mountain became my reality.

It was there, sitting at my sweet little patio table with my dog at my feet, completely in love with my life, that I decided that THIS is my purpose! I wanted to teach other women how to achieve this kind of happiness and spare them the ups and downs and spectacular failures of my own journey. I dubbed myself a "Happiness Coach" (I thought I made up that term!) and Be Happy First was born!

Now, I have a new dream, of a lodge and retreat center right here in these amazing mountains. Hosting meditation retreats and introducing people to the joys of wandering around in a temperate rainforest. I want another retreat in a tropical location, maybe on the beach, maybe on Lake Atitlan in Guatemala, a place I fell in love with. I love my life and I am so excited and expectant of the amazing things that are coming next. I love dreaming and watching those dreams manifest. I love figuring out ways to get this message to the women who are really yearning for and ready for it. Happiness is a choice! Learn how to choose happiness! Be Happy First and everything else will fall into place in perfect time.

ABOUT THE AUTHOR: Lauren G. Foster is an author, speaker, Happiness Teacher, certified Meditation Teacher, Primal Health Coach, Life Mastery Consultant, and Dream Builder Coach. She started Be Happy First in 2014 and is on a mission to help one million women learn to be Happy and Free on Purpose before her sixtieth birthday in 2025. When she's not writing, producing the *How to Choose Happiness and Freedom Show*, or creating teaching tools, she can be found hiking and basking in the woods with her two dogs and four cats near her mountainside home in the Appalachian Mountains of East Tennessee.

Lauren G. Foster
Be Happy First
behappyfirst.buzzsprout.com
Lauren@behappyfirst.org
931-841-8045

I Am More Than My Body
Jackie Garfield

When we are children, we don't give our bodies much thought. We run and play with abundant energy until we collapse in a heap at the end of the day. We don't question whether our body will be there for us or do as we ask. Our body and mind operate as one, partners in our day to day adventures. Then the day comes when our body is singled out, suddenly a separate entity from the rest of us. Perhaps it was when the well-meaning relative criticized our chubby belly, or we perused health magazines only to discover we looked nothing like the models who were the "picture of health."

I learned my body was valuable when I was thirteen. I was one of the first girls in my class to develop, growing to a C cup by the seventh grade. One afternoon I was hanging out at the roller skating rink when a friend introduced me to his uncle. After slowly checking me out from head to toe, he remarked, "I can see why you like her." It wasn't just what he said, but how he said it—like he was a predator, eying his prey. I felt dirty and shameful, like I had done something wrong. I was too young to understand that he was the one who should have been ashamed and, for the first time in my life, I was acutely aware of my body and its effect on others.

Around the same time, I began to get a lot of attention from some of the boys in my class. There were crude comments made about my newly-defined curves and clumsy attempts to get a hug or otherwise physically closer to me. It was uninvited and unwanted, but these teenaged boys were impulsive and insensitive. My comfort was inconsequential to their hormones. None of this went unnoticed by the girls in my class, and the next thing I knew I was unceremoniously kicked out of my group of friends and made the outcast. I didn't know what I had done wrong, but I knew that I didn't want to feel like my body was more important than the rest of me, so I started covering up. Baggy t-shirts and oversized flannels were my favorite. To this day former classmates comment on these staples from my wardrobe. Mission accomplished.

In high school, I first learned what dieting was. I grew up in a health-conscious household, so I was taught about "healthy" and "unhealthy" foods. While we never formally dieted, I wasn't allowed sugary cereals, and we didn't have much snacky food in the house. It was a friend who educated me on dieting, namely, that it was important to exercise and eat a low-fat diet. I'll never forget the day we went rollerblading along the lakefront for several hours, then stopped for large, soft breadsticks at the local pizza shop. Without a thought to portion control, we gorged ourselves and still felt good because, hey, it was low-fat! While I didn't diet with her at the time, the seed had been planted.

Fast-forward to freshman year of college. Now on my own, with the freedom to eat whatever I wanted, I indulged in all the foods I wasn't allowed to have growing up. I didn't give this behavior much thought until I went home for the summer carrying an extra twenty pounds. My parents expressed concern and I was beginning to feel self-conscious about the extra weight, so I went on my first diet. Thanks to my high school friend, I already had some idea of how to lose weight. I limited my calories and fat grams and worked out for an hour every day. The pounds melted off easily.

When I got back to school, everyone noticed and praised me for my slimmed-down figure. I looked great! While I enjoyed the renewed attention, particularly from boys, I was again reminded that my body and its size mattered. What about my summer spent working my first professional job and building the skills I would eventually take into the working world? That mattered too, but it was my body that stole the show. Eventually I ditched my reduced-calorie diet and resumed eating what I liked, though I kept up the exercise routine which, for a time, helped keep my weight in check.

Then came my next big life transition, from college student to Corporate America. I was still eating what I liked, but now, instead of running around campus all day I was sitting at a desk. Before I knew it, I was back up to my post-freshman-year weight. How had this happened? Back on a diet I went. This time around, the weight loss didn't come so easily. And so a cycle was born. Over the next decade, I would gain and lose the same ten to fifteen pounds over and over again.

Throughout all these dieting attempts, I never stopped to ask myself why I kept doing what was recommended and not getting results that were promised. I blamed myself and, more notably, my body, for the inevitable weight regain. I also didn't ask myself why it was so important to be a certain weight, a smaller size. I believed that smaller was better, despite my body telling me over and over that it wasn't meant to be. Instead, I saw my body as the enemy. I blamed it for everything. I avoided being seen in a swimsuit because my body didn't look the way it should, the way it could. I didn't like having pictures taken because there was always a flaw to pick apart. And I certainly couldn't date, because the men I wanted didn't want someone who was overweight. No, it was better to wait until I lost weight to start living.

Despite my resistance to dating, I did find love. He loved my body just as it was and told me so often. Soon I started to see what he saw and appreciate some parts of my body. But the war was still on. He also introduced me to the last diet I would ever try: the now ever-popular low-carb diet. The science behind it made sense. The application, however, left me feeling more out of control around food than I ever had before. I couldn't have any of the things I enjoy: pasta, bread, ice cream. Because I couldn't resist these treats for long, I would binge and have to restart my low-carb "lifestyle" a dozen times. It wasn't sustainable and yet I continued to see myself as the problem.

My moment of truth came when, fresh out of that relationship, I had a decision to make. Was I going to stress over the pounds that needed to be lost before dating again, or would I finally accept myself as whole, just as I was? I knew I couldn't go on dieting, obsessing about food, and never fully committing to my exercise routine because none of it felt good to me. For the first time in ages, I heard my body whisper. And I listened. I stopped dieting for good. As it would turn out, that was the easy part.

Now that I wasn't actively trying to change my body, I was left with another decision. There was a possibility that I would be this weight for the rest of my life. Could I be okay with that? Could I let go of a lifetime of trying to be smaller and just be me, without the endless pursuit of weight loss? If so, a huge shift was going to be in order. I was going to have to change how I viewed my body. I could no longer talk badly about myself. I had to build a practice of gratitude for all the things my body does for me day in and day out. I had to be intentional about truly seeing and appreciating what was attractive and beautiful about my body. I also had to let go of what my body "could" look like.

The shift didn't happen overnight. I had to forgive those who had hurt me with insensitive comments, then I had to forgive myself for letting it affect me for as long as I did. I also had to forgive myself for the misguided dieting decisions I made in the pursuit of happiness. Most importantly, I focused on all of the beautiful qualities that make me unique as a human, which, as it turned out, had nothing to do with my body. I'm generous and kind. Intelligent and funny. These are the things people think of when they think about me. Not my dress size.

After making peace with myself, I suddenly had all this energy to direct my disgust at the true enemy, the dieting and advertising industries. And I got MAD AS HELL. They'd preyed on me. They saw my insecurities and subtly twisted it for their profit. They'd never wanted me to succeed, because if I felt inadequate and self-conscious I would keep buying their products. And I had bought it, hook, line, and sinker…until now. I know too much and will never again give away my power to some nameless, faceless person whose approval I'll never win. Because the truth is, the only person who needs to approve is ME.

My first test came when I decided I needed headshots for my new business. I worried about the flaws that would be captured for eternity but I felt the fear and did it anyway. It was one the most liberating things I've ever done for myself. My photographer was amazing and when we reviewed the photos together, I cried. It was like I was seeing myself for the first time. I had told myself I wasn't enough for so long that I'd missed what was right in front of me. I felt empowered and confident—more confident than I'd ever felt in my whole life. Some of these photos would eventually make it to my online dating profile, and the light in my eyes and smile would attract my future husband.

While I've come a long way, I know there will still be challenges. I still live in a world where I am bombarded 24/7 with images of women who look nothing like me, and I'm sold a vision of a life that could be. I have to remind myself regularly of my decision to live body-shame-free. I was tested again when I had my engagement photos taken. I felt great. It was a beautiful day and we had some amazing shots on the lake at sunset. I couldn't wait to see them, but when the reveal day came my heart sank. I didn't look the way I'd felt inside. I immediately saw all the flaws I've been trained to see: the unflattering angles, my round belly, the back fat. As these old, conditioned thoughts raced through my head, I made another decision. I could allow these old thoughts and beliefs about what is unattractive ruin my engagement celebration, or I could choose to see the beauty in those pictures. There was the undeniable love my fiancé and I have for one another and the joy we felt in celebrating the beginning of our lives together. I also reminded myself that my fiancé loves every curve on my body and he didn't see any of the flaws I saw.

The truth about transformation is that it's a journey. There are little moments that guide you to your truth, if you have the guts to listen. My moments are too many to count, but once I started honoring myself instead of all the outside voices telling me what I should want and how I should feel, I was free. I have found a sense of peace and freedom I could have never imagined just a few short years ago. My mind is calm. I am present to what is happening right now, not what might be one day. I now expend my energy on things that bring me joy and I love my body, just as it is.

ABOUT THE AUTHOR: Jackie Garfield is a certified Intuitive Eating Counselor and body image coach. She is passionate about helping women ditch the diets to make peace with food and their bodies. As a recovering corporate worker-bee who worked in finance for a Fortune 100 company for over twelve years, Jackie loves watching what unfolds for her clients when they create more space to live an authentic and aligned life. She obtained her Health & Mastery Coaching certificates from the Health Coach Institute. When she's not busy creating change for her clients, Jackie loves hanging out with her husband and stepdaughter.

Jackie Garfield
Health & Wellness Coaching
jackiegarfield.com
contact@jackiegarfield.com

Moving Past Fear and Into Courage

Andrea Firpo

I woke up to heaviness, an intense pressure behind my eyes, and a familiar ache in my face. I was physically and emotionally depleted; hollow, sullen. The result of yet another night silencing my sobs in the bathtub. Before I even got out of bed the thoughts began racing; thoughts surrounding my husband, his treatment of me, and what had become of our relationship.

Just recently he had announced he wanted to fly to Brazil to meet his online girlfriend. It was as if the floor had dropped out beneath me. What if he never came back? How was I going to explain this to our fifteen-year-old daughter? To our friends and family?

More importantly, how would I continue to keep it (and by "it" I mean our open marriage) a secret?

It would have been one thing if I was happy with this arrangement, but I wasn't, not anymore. My marriage had become something completely outside of what was comfortable for me, yet I had continued to allow it because I was committed to making things work and keeping a stable homelife for our daughter.

I clawed my way out of bed, silently rejecting and resenting the day ahead as I stumbled to the bathroom to get ready for work. My daughter would need help making her lunch, and I needed to figure out how to hold it together until she went to school.

Sucking in a breath, I looked in the bathroom mirror and was surprised to see that my left eye was puffy, its eyelid wrinkly like crepe paper. I couldn't quite put my finger on what was wrong. I turned to my husband, who was also getting ready for work, and said, "Do you see that?"

"Do I see what?"

I pointed to my eye. "*That.*"

He squinted, examining me, and said after a quick assessment, "It's just swollen."

Trying to keep it light, I winked at him. "Yeah, I'm probably just getting old!"

I saw him wince with discomfort at my joke, then turned back to the mirror and my left eye. I wasn't imagining things. My eyes had been swollen before, but they had never looked like this.

My age, and its effect on my marriage, was just another thing I was struggling with. My husband loved the chase, and while I kept getting older the girls he pursued stayed the same age. Even worse, he seemed to fall a little bit harder for each one. Some days I felt I had to work so hard just to get a moment of his attention.

As I turned on the water and stepped into the shower, he lightly patted my bottom, then joined me. I let the heat of it consume me and wash away what I was feeling. Nothing was going to change.

That evening we had plans to go out with Chrissy and Mark, friends with whom we'd experienced a fair share of life. Chrissy also felt the enormous pressure to keep up the show for our men, managing their happiness while simultaneously soaking our wounds in alcohol.

On the weekends, Mark and Chrissy prided themselves on going out to bars and picking up women to sleep with. Incredibly competitive, Mark was always flashing pictures in my husband's face to show him what he had missed out on. My husband never failed to take the bait, and I couldn't help but think the envy fueled his extramarital pursuits. Yet I knew he was genuinely attached to both Chrissy and Mark, and, as it so happened, the couple they'd invited to join us that night.

I noticed him stare at the stunning brunette seated in the booth next to her partner; I also watched their reactions as we introduced ourselves and knew there was nothing I could do. Resigned, I turned to Chrissy, and with my voice lowered asked, "Do you see anything weird going on with my left eye?"

While getting ready that night, my eye glared at me again as I put on my makeup. As always, I applied the thick black line, but now it seemed like my eye was screaming, *"Look at me!"*

I'd caught my husband's gaze in the mirror, pointed to my eye and snapped, "Do you really not see *that*?"

"Let me see," he said, gentle and patient.

I stepped towards him and looked into his brown and orange-flecked eyes, trusting that maybe he could see what I could see.

"Andrea," he said, still looking at me though quickly losing interest, "maybe you see something because it's *your* face, but I don't. I honestly don't see anything wrong with you."

I felt like a crazy bitch, but not too crazy to ask Chrissy about it.

She took a sip of her red wine and laughed, "Oh, Andrea! What are you talking about? You are *gorrrr-geousss!* You always look stunning!"

I frowned at her answer and couldn't shake my unease. I asked my esthetician. My coworkers. No one saw it. I dropped it.

Six months later, I took a trip to see my mother, who within thirty seconds of my arrival looked at me sharply and said, "Andrea… what is going on with your eye?"

My jaw fell open. *"You can see that?"* I couldn't believe that after all this time someone was finally validating my concern. "Everyone told me it was nothing! No one else could see what I saw, and I just thought I was making things up!"

"Of course I see it," she said with a roll of her eyes, "I am *your* mother. I know everything about you."

The irony of her statement wasn't lost on me, as she had no idea what was going on in my life. At least now I knew I needed to see a doctor.

Within a month I had a diagnosis. "Don't google it," my doctor said as I was leaving the office, "Just make an appointment to see me in two weeks."

I waited until I got on the bus, then pulled out my phone and searched "Graves' Disease." The images I saw brought me to tears.

Graves' Disease is an autoimmune condition that attacks the thyroid tissue, which begins to swell. Your body also thinks the tissue behind your eye is identical to your thyroid tissue. The inflammation presses so hard on your optic nerve, your eye bulges out of your face.

I was close to the point of no return and even in danger of losing my eyesight. Both my endocrinologist and ophthalmologist wanted me to remove my thyroid and go on medication for the rest of my life.

I told them no, and remained resolute no matter how they persisted.

Turning to everyone I knew, I tearfully shared my story. A co-worker recommended a nutritional counselor. During our consultation, he had me put on an apron, then muscle tested me for minerals, putting the tiny vials of the ones I needed in the pockets of the apron.

"Why would you ever choose to be sick and need medication for the rest of your life," he asked, "when you could just be healthy?"

I didn't know if it was the weight of his words or the weight of my apron, but for the first time I felt hopeful. Appreciative of his guidance, I said, "You're hired."

I went home that day with a dizzying amount of supplements and minerals. A few days later, a yoga teacher who lived in my building told me, "You should really go get attuned to Pranashakthi. I know the most *amazing* teacher teaching a class at my studio!"

I had no idea what energy work was, but I was desperate and willing to try anything. Intuitively, I knew something big had to happen.

During my next appointment, my acupuncturist said to me in his heavy German accent, "You know, in Europe, if you really want to heal yourself, we recommend a lifestyle change." Listening to him, I felt like I was washed clean. I took a deep inhalation and heard the word inside me loud and clear: *Portland.*

Moving to Portland from San Francisco felt impossible. *How was I going to make that happen*?

For the past eight years I'd regularly suggested the idea of moving to Portland to both my daughter and my husband, only to be met with blank stares and unenthusiastic responses.

Five years prior, and in reaction to seeing my husband's secret profile on a dating site, I packed bags for my daughter and I, picked her up from school, and started the ten-hour drive to Portland. We stayed with my best friend from college for three weeks, during which our house, which had already been listed, sold in one of the largest economic downturns this country had ever seen. The sale meant we automatically rolled into a contract for an offer on a house in San Francisco—the purchase already negotiated and contingent upon the sale.

Instead of seeing our house selling as a way out and staying in Portland, I limply renegotiated the terms of our marriage and came back to San Francisco with my tail between my legs. I felt I had no other choice. My daughter wouldn't get out of bed or talk to me. When she finally did speak, she begged me to go back home.

Worse yet, I was a terrible negotiator. Terrified of standing up for myself and losing the person who knew me better than anyone in my life, I asked for very little. But now, I could no longer keep my side of the bargain. I knew I was killing myself.

A few weeks after my acupuncture appointment, I stood on the Streetcar platform, waiting to take the train into work and listening to my husband and his best friend complain about their boss.

Suddenly, and as if he could hear my thoughts, he said, "Maybe I should quit, and we can sell our house and move to Portland."

I called our realtor that day. But when I told my husband, I was met with a brick wall.

"Woah, woah, woah…" he said, as if this was a new idea. "What are you doing, Andrea? We *live* here. My job is here!"

"We need to start over," I replied. "We need to burn down everything and rebuild it if we are going to stay together."

"What are you talking about?" Shaking his head in exasperation, he walked towards the stairs, away from me. "When will you ever be happy with what you have?"

I turned my head towards the windows so he wouldn't see the tears forming, but I knew *he knew* I was crying. I glued the words together in a rush, voice wobbling, "I need to start over. I need to change everything. The psychics during my reading told me. I am off of my life path –"

He cut me off with a huff. "Oh *good*, Andrea. You win for crying!"

I heard it again, louder this time: *Portland*. It was definitive and rang with truth. I heard myself say, "We need to move to Portland. *I* am moving to Portland. You are welcome to join me."

"How is that going to work?" he snapped back, seething now and having no problem hiding his resentment, challenging me with the very question I had asked myself.

Weakened, I looked down again. "I don't know." Even as I said the words, I knew that if I didn't make it happen, I was sure to regret it.

Moments after we sold our home, I gave notice at my job. I didn't know what was next, but I knew with every part of my being that I had made the right decision. I had willingly blown up my life, but I felt the expansion to create something new in its place.

I let go of all of my friends, my career, the late night parties, the "lifestyle", and everything else I had outgrown. I mostly let go of who I was supposed to be. I researched my disease, and drastically changed my diet. I continued to see great energy healers and holistic practitioners who patiently led, held, and guided me on my darkest days. I learned how to make peace with being in the awkward space between my past and future—not always seeing a way forward.

I kept swimming until I found the shore. I even filed for divorce.

One year later, I was healed, and living in Portland, Oregon.

I did it. I made it happen.

ABOUT THE AUTHOR: Andrea Firpo is a Psychic Cheerleader focused on transformational healing by building awareness in the body and mind around the deep conditioning of emotional trauma. Andrea draws from her background in psychology, feng shui, plant medicine, reiki, shamanism, and psychic energetic healing to identify underlying patterns that undermine her clients' self-worth. The simple yet powerful energetic tools she teaches helps them identify blocks, expand their intuition, heal, and make incredible paradigm shifts in their lives. Andrea also highlights the stories of incredible women in her podcast, "Brilliance through Resilience." She lives with her family in Portland, Oregon and works with clients everywhere.

Andrea Firpo
Andrea Firpo, Psychic Cheerleader
psychiccheerleader.com
andrea@andreafirpo.com
415-300-5848

Transcending the Trauma Trap
From Terror to Triumph
Shelora Fitzgerald

W hen the chance to have my transformational story published in this anthology presented itself, I was beyond thrilled. I have been trying to have my story heard for many years. Now, I actually had a chance of being published!

As 'Inspector Joe Friday' used to say, "Just the facts ma'am." Here are the facts.

When I was nine years old, a fifteen-year-old boy, in an effort to prove his manhood, attempted to rape me in the woods. Overnight, I turned from a trusting, confident, adventurous, imaginative child into a traumatized victim. I shrank into a timid, insecure, inhibited, self-conscious child, full of anxiety, guilt, and shame. Once friendly, outgoing, and carefree, I now ran away in terror from familiar figures, even the friendly milkman.

When the innocence of a child is attacked, fragments of her shattered Soul take refuge in the Light, leaving behind a void filled with dark entities whose sole purpose is the murder of that Soul.

It was not until I was sixty-six years old, that a specialist diagnosed me with a particularly severe combination of trauma-induced ADHD, PTSD, OCD, and Bipolar II Disorder.

The doctor told me that the traumatic assault I had experienced in my childhood had permanently injured my mind, body, and Soul in ways that had seriously hampered my ability to function successfully in the world.

He explained how, when under attack, the brain disassociates itself from the pain of trauma by walling itself off into separate compartments.

He said the executive function of my pre-frontal lobe was permanently damaged. This is the part of the brain that plans, organizes, problem solves, and executes. Under stress (PTSD) the original trauma is triggered. Everything appears equally critical, making it virtually impossible for me to prioritize. Thus, a deadline occurs for me literally as a "DEAD-line."

It was only then that I fully realized the devastation that shocking incident had wreaked on all aspects of my life.

The diagnosis helped me to finally understand the source of the destructive emotional and psychological patterns of behavior that had ruined my career, my finances, and my relationships. They had been hardwired into my brain, unbeknownst to me, and had been running the show all my life. In a doctor's note, he said, "On her best days she is brilliant. On her worst, she is barely able to perform normal, everyday tasks. What takes others two weeks can take her two months."

As a result, instead of the theatre career I longed for, I created drama in my personal life. Instead of peaceful, productive, stable relationships, I provoked conflict to create the clarity and focus provided by adrenaline when in the "fight" mode. Not surprisingly, I had racked up two failed marriages.

You could say that my life has been an endless string of breakdowns, incomplete projects, missed deadlines and opportunities, financial calamities, endless legal battles, harmful accidents, and conflicted relationships. I have been scammed, beaten, cheated, robbed, and disinherited. My impulsive choices have cost me hundreds of thousands of dollars and countless opportunities.

I liken this to the tsunami of terror currently sweeping this planet, wreaking havoc. It is as if both hemispheres of the World's brain are addicted to adrenaline, survival, fear, just like the brain of a traumatized child.

I wanted my story to show that, despite all the drama, chaos, and cruelty; the fear and the fighting; the greed and the grift; the addiction to violence; the mad pursuit of fool's gold to fill the hollow hearts of those who have never known the embrace of unconditional love and acceptance—the world is virtually dying for love.

Down the Rabbit Hole

I set about writing immediately. I had about two weeks and two thousand words in which to do it. I was determined to meet the deadline.

I wrote every day, from ten in the morning, until two or three in the morning. I put in literally hundreds of hours, "down the rabbit hole," writing, rewriting, editing as I went. I would spend an hour or more on a single paragraph, laboring diligently to find exactly the perfect word, phrase, image, metaphor, or simile, arranging and rearranging, trying to find the perfect order for each sentence.

Yet here I was again, way past my deadline, going around in circles, going nowhere fast. I could not see the finish line.

It felt like a train wreck in slow motion. Even though I understood what was happening, I couldn't make it stop. I was furious with myself, stomping around my house, yelling, "Are you crazy? What is the matter with you? This is the chance you've been waiting for. Why are you sabotaging yourself, *again?*"

I was up against that ancient traumatic wound, caught in what I call the "trauma trap."

Reflecting my breakdown, all three of my computers malfunctioned. The day after the deadline, my cursor completely disappeared, leaving me unable to save or send the document I had so painstakingly prepared!

Finally, after five hours of tech support, I put my foot down and said to the Universe, "ENOUGH! I have done everything I know to fix this by myself. None of it is working! I am about to lose the opportunity of a lifetime. I refuse to lose this fight! I will not let this beat me. It has ruined my life! I'm not going to give up. This is too important to me. It's my turn! I need a miracle. And I need it right now!"

The nature of trauma is to protect yourself so that you can't even allow yourself to know what you really desire.

I had learned to be a good performer. I did what was expected of me. I had become an actress, adept at expressing other people's truths.

I knew if I could do the hard work of feeling all the grief and the rage locked inside my body, I would find myself free to feel my own feelings and desires.

That is where my story was, in my body, not in my head. I had been editing myself to death, obsessed with perfection.

In the most ironic of plot twists, I realized I had been editing myself out of my own story. I had put a gag order on myself, had left my truth on the cutting room floor.

In that moment, I allowed myself to surrender to the truth of who I really am, and the purpose of my own life, and to stop paying the penalty I had paid all my life.

There was a real penalty to knowing the truth.

But I demanded to finally be allowed to be heard, seen, and felt, to connect with the audience I had dreamed of all my life, and to be received, not as a performer, but as my authentic self.

I sat down and wrote my way out of hell, telling my story from the power of truth inside my body.

Innocence Lost

I have spent a lifetime healing the crack that opened up in my soul when that broken, angry young man brutally assaulted me. Though, by the Grace of God, I managed to talk him out of actually raping me, he made it clear that he could just as easily have killed me. The daggers of his murderous rage, hatred, guilt, and blame penetrated my nine-year-old body and took root in my heart and mind leaving invisible scars which have taken a lifetime to heal. That day, my attacker was taken away in handcuffs, while I was left to face a very different kind of prison.

The Enchanted Forest

As a skinny young girl with bright blue eyes and a mop of curly white-blonde hair, I carried myself with the lightness and grace of a natural born dancer. I could swim in water over my head and loved to play with boys because they had *way* more fun and *way* better adventures than girls did.

One fine day, I slipped into my yellow bathing suit and asked my babysitter if I could go into the woods to meet a boy and his friends at a swimming hole. She gave her consent, too busy resisting the advances of a fifteen-year-old "greaser" to give it much thought.

Unfortunately, the greaser she was flirting with was paying rapt attention. He needed to f**k someone in order to gain admission to a gang. As I danced my way happily through Sherwood Forest, pretending I was Maid Marian on my way to meet Robin Hood and his Band of Merry Men, he followed stealthily, waiting for his chance to pounce. His opportunity came when I stopped, spellbound by two white butterflies dancing in a ray of light in the forest. From behind the bushes, he watched as I tiptoed into the light beam and stood so still that the butterflies, mistaking me for a flower, gently came to rest on top of my head.

Heaven on Earth.

The shimmering, perfect purity of that moment of grace was so powerful, it has been a beacon of light I can always return to for sanctuary.

What happened next is engraved in my memory forever.

Just seconds later, the spell was broken by an assault on my innocence so devastating; it totally upended and transformed the course of my life forever. The two together tell the story of my before and after, of joy and terror, of innocence lost and regained.

The Greaser in the Woods

The spell was broken by the sharp "crack," of a branch breaking in the woods. It sliced through the sacred silence like a knife, letting me know that I was not alone.

A "greaser" in full uniform, oily black hair slicked back in a "duck's tail," sauntered out of the woods and sidled up beside me. He lit a cigarette, took a long drag, then he dropped it and ground it out under his heel, as if warning me, "I could extinguish you too, just like that."

Next thing I knew, I was flat on my back with a knee in my groin, pinned to the ground like a beautiful butterfly with a stake through its heart. His face was contorted with rage, spittle foaming out of the corners of its mouth, like a rabid dog.

Through clenched teeth, he spat his curse.

"I'm gonna *F**K* you!"

I didn't know what "f**k" was. From my innocence, I blurted, "What's f**k?"

It was as if I could hear his thoughts: "What a f**king loser! She doesn't even know what 'f**k' is!"

Whatever it was, he didn't really want it.

Suddenly he seemed trapped under the ice in a pond, screaming for someone to break through and save him from drowning.

His pain pierced my heart with compassion.

I would be his someone.

I reached for truth.

"I have a father who loves me very much. If you let me go, he will give you money."

As if in a movie, I could see his father, staggering drunk, screaming insults and swinging punches at his son's face. His mother stood by powerless, in the background.

In that moment, I understood.

My father loved me. His father hated him.

He was poor. I was not.

His answer said it all.

"How much?"

"I don't know, but a lot!"

He loosened his grip.

"Can I go now?"

He jerked his head dismissively.

"Yeah, you can go."

Some inexplicable power had helped me save that young man from his worst self, and in so doing, I had saved myself.

A Necklace of Miracles

For every crash and burn there has been an equally powerful

miraculous moment that lit up the dark night sky of my soul like fireworks and saved my life, again, just as it did that day in the woods.

That truth is, my life has been threaded together, miracle by miracle, like a beautiful strand of luminous pearls, a tiny knot painstakingly tied between each one, as if by an invisible hand, to protect it from being damaged by friction with its neighbor and strengthen the entire strand.

A pearl necklace is clasped together by what they call a catch.

Have you noticed that there always seems to be a catch?

Well here it is:

It can take years for the irritation of a tiny grain of sand to grow, slowly, layer upon luminous layer, into a pearl. Perhaps those tiny little knots of pain are the grains of sand required to irritate the miraculous growth of pearls. They also serve to strengthen and protect the beauty of a necklace of miracles, so it can become an enduring heirloom, a legacy of miracles, passed down from generation to generation, each one adding its own precious miracles to the silk thread that runs through their lives, clasping the stories of their lives together.

ABOUT THE AUTHOR: Shelora's escape from attempted rape at the age of nine drives her lifelong quest to understand the nature of God. Along the way, she has acquired a vast array of historical, scientific, psychological, and metaphysical knowledge, tools, and techniques. A highly intuitive spiritual teacher and creative visionary, Shelora has a rich background in the performing and healing arts. She runs the gamut from actress and director to Registered Clinical Counselor, Course in Miracles therapist and Soul Psychologist. Now a public speaker, she inspires her audiences to recognize the hidden treasure trove of precious gifts buried beneath every traumatic wound.

Shelora Fitzgerald, M. Ed., R.C.C.
Registered Clinical Counsellor
Soul Psychologist & Advanced Hand Analyst
shelora.com
inspiration@shelora.com

Awakening Stillness
Becki Lanham

I wasn't sure what to expect as I sat crossed-legged on the bamboo floor alongside six other women that first day of class. As a massage therapist, I had taken many continuing education classes over the past decade, but this somehow felt different. Spread across the table at the front of the room was an array of anatomy and women's health books, a flexible cloth pelvis, a vase of vibrant flowers, a small clay pot billowing with the earthy fragrance of smoldering copal incense, and a set of pink life-sized clay uterus models. The room felt warm and cozy, quite like a womb itself, especially in comparison to the biting cold of that early February morning.

The instructor began by inviting us to speak our intentions for attending The Arvigo Techniques of Maya Abdominal Therapy® self-care workshop. As each woman expressed her desire to deepen self-care practices, fortify physical and emotional healing journeys, and strengthen the connection with her feminine body, I listened in astonishment. As someone who had long worshiped at the temple of productivity and perfectionism, I couldn't understand why someone would invest energy, finances, and three full days away from responsibilities at home simply for the purpose of exploring self-care.

When it was my turn to voice my intention, I spoke with pride, feeling far more centered in a purpose of proficiency than the women around me.

"I'm here so that I can move onto the next two trainings to become certified and begin to utilize abdominal therapy within my practice."

The Arvigo Institute required every potential practitioner to first attend a self-care training to deepen the understanding of the work through their own experiences before stepping into the role of care provider for others. Essentially, I was there to complete the prerequisite to learning a useful and profitable skill. However, by the end of the training it would become clear that my well-calculated business investment was actually a divinely guided journey so that I could experience a softening within myself and unlocking of my life's purpose.

As the long weekend unfolded, moments of rest, teaching of self-care practices, and meditations were peppered throughout the educational lectures. It was within these pauses, as well as the exceptionally rare nights spent in solitude, that I was given the invitation and sacred space to be still. This was in complete polarity to my usual fast-paced and perfectly planned busyness. There were no moments of stillness at home, I made sure of that. My lifelong rituals of productivity had become my primary measure of self-worth. I often pushed through the exhaustion that accompanies overproduction to silence any internal doubt that I was good enough, in control, and efficient in meeting the social and self-inflicted expectations within my roles as businessowner, health provider, homemaker, wife, mother, daughter, sister, and friend. Exhaustion aside, this endless movement secured a feeling of control within my life and that control provided me comfort.

As the end the second day of the workshop approached, the instructor asked us to get comfortable in preparation for a guided meditation. I settled onto the floor, surrounded by the shuffling sounds of other women arranging themselves in anticipation of the upcoming silence. The overhead lights were dimmed until the room was illuminated only by the dull glow of the crescent moon shining through the windows. As I closed my eyes, I felt myself finally beginning to trust the stillness that had felt so foreign just a few days prior. As my body slowly let go to be cradled by the floor, the subtle sounds of the room became distant. Snuggled safely in a blanket like a caterpillar in her chrysalis, I rested my warm, open palms on my belly, feeling them rise and fall with each slow and mindful breath. I intuitively began using the familiar language of intentional touch that I had become so practiced at during my years serving others. As my hands tenderly embraced what felt like the most vulnerable part of myself, I began to speak with my body, not with the typical overbearing and one-sided voice of self-judgement, resentment, and demands of compliancy, but rather a hushed tone with messages of acceptance and gratitude. Moved by a growing willingness to listen, a long-locked door within my heart opened and I began to silently hold space to allow my body to speak.

I was surprised at how quiet and timid her voice was. She reminded me of a withdrawn, wounded child, unsteady within her speech after years of being silenced. She first whispered of her heavy grief for the loss of the daughter, placed for adoption after birth, whom she so tenderly loved and patiently nurtured in utero. She shared her guilt and shame from a sexual assault at age sixteen and her confusion with the silence that followed. She felt like a failure for being unable to meet the impossibly high expectations for her to look and perform in a way that was not of her true nature. I heard the fragility in her voice as she wept of how damaged and worthless she felt through the years of sexualization as her leading mark of worthiness. As she spoke, I sensed the landscape of unfertile ground that had separated us for so long lying just underneath my open hands, within in the softness of my belly. There was a pain that resided there, but also a budding homecoming of joy in the recognition that I may finally be able to reclaim her as my own again.

As the meditation continued and my connection with her deepened, that dry ground began to crack open and an underground spring of long-suppressed emotions flowed up from my belly, bubbled into my heart and throat, and manifested as warm tears that spilled uncontrollably down my face, soaking into my hair spread wildly around me.

I was still processing the meditation the next morning as I stood in the stark white bathroom, still steamy from my shower, and readied myself for the final day of class. As the fog gradually lifted, I paused my daily routine to stare curiously into the large mirror. Reflected back at me was a renewed image of myself, a pure source of beauty luminous in the bright glow from the vanity lights. I was taken aback as I felt an expanding wave of love for her, the same warming love that rose when I looked down into my two-year-old son's smiling face, held my husband's strong and callused hands, or snuggled with my beloved fluffy dog. The love that had always so easily poured from me to others was, for the first time that I could remember, flowing from me and circling back to fill my own heart. Suddenly it clicked: this was the feeling that should be present within my self-care practices. Until now, my perception of self-care had been a neatly typed and printed checklist hanging on my refrigerator. As I checked off each task, I satisfied my need to feel productive and came one step closer to fixing what I viewed as unsightly brokenness within myself. As I stood in front of that mirror, I began to understand that, regardless of how healthy the activity seemed, preforming self-care that was based in feelings of inadequacy was not caring for myself in the slightest. The self-care practices I would bring home with me would ultimately flourish into nourishing rituals full of mindfulness that I choose to do intentionally because I loved myself and knew that I deserved to be treated with affection and admiration.

The morning I returned home, I was brimming with an excited energy to embrace my family and share all that had been awakened within me. I couldn't tell if it was the crescendo of heat from the rising sun or the newfound brightness from within that warmed me as I carried my suitcase down the sideway toward my front door. A passing neighbor, bundled tightly to shield herself from the cold morning air, flashed a smile and said, "You look radiant! You have a bit of a sparkle in your eyes." She confirmed what I had already known: a fire had been lit within my heart and was shining its radiance through my full being to the outside world.

In the days that followed, I began restructuring my home and work schedules to set aside daily pauses to continue the mutual and compassionate communication I had begun with my body. It was within these moments that I quickly realized that she had been trying to speak to me for years by sending up the red flags of irregular cycles, excessive bleeding, and crippling period pain. It had been mentioned during the workshop that period pain was not a genetic curse we were born to bear but rather a sign of dysfunction and ,with the correct care, the pain could be eliminated. I had little faith in these words, however. Maybe they could prove true for anyone else, but certainly not me, who for nearly two decades had spent two to three full days each month curled in bed with labor-like waves of pain and nausea. Now that I was actively expanding my mind-body connection and had centered my self-care practices in self-love, the red flags were immediately lowered. To my utter astonishment, just one week after returning home, I experienced a completely pain-free period for the first time in my life.

Although my moments of enlightenment were tangible and instantaneous, my true transformation did not happen overnight. I walked through the following years healing my surfaced traumas and gently reshaping my life practices one small step at a time. Eventually, my body's voice was no longer frail and fearful but powerful, confident, and serene. I learned to intuitively trust her and her innate wisdom. Additionally, as I surrendered my white-knuckled grip on productivity and control I saw it for what it really was: a constant white noise that was silencing my emotions and invalidating my experiences. As that noise retreated, it became easier for me to see my life experiences as significant lessons in growth rather than challenging obstacles interfering with a meticulously fine-tuned life plan.

After the awakenings within my self-care training and the first pain-free period that followed, I could see with total clarity my calling toward a career in holistic women's wellness. The newly lit fire within me fueled my devotion to plant the same seeds of self-love and self-acceptance that I had been graciously gifted into the hearts of other women. I have since dedicated my life to learning and sharing all I can to help cultivate the collective change necessary to reawaken the long-forgotten power of stillness in a culture that exclusively values continuous productivity. For it is only through surrendering to the dark and unmoving tranquility of the chrysalis that we are able to discover the life-altering transformation that we had no idea we were even looking for.

ABOUT THE AUTHOR: Becki joyfully serves women through her holistic practice nestled in the beautiful Shenandoah Valley of Virginia. She offers an array of services: Arvigo® Abdominal Therapy sessions, health coaching, birth and bereavement doula services, as well as Arvigo® Therapy self-care classes and other feminine-focused workshops. Her ever-growing passion for sharing holistic women's wellness services and education with others has led her to her most recent venture—expanding her education to become certified as both a Fertility Awareness Educator and Sexual and Reproductive Health Educator.

Becki Lanham
Hands with Heart
handswithheart.net
becki@handswithheart.net
540-539-7227

The Awakening by Light, Love & Fire
Darnell Florane Gouzy

My transformation began in 1992, when I got into an auto accident that left me with severe physical injuries. For six long years I was stuck in a loop of hopelessness and despair as I struggled with pain and depression, with no end in sight. Then I realized that the more I ruminated over my pain, dysfunction, and depression, the more intense they became. I knew that I had to release them in order to transform and grow.

That "tragic" accident would turn out to be the most pivotal moment in my life. And as my own life began its awakening by light, love, and fire, I became acutely aware of the suffering of others that I had not noticed before. I developed a greater and deeper sense of compassion, hope, and love.

Over the next twenty-eight years, my soul's purpose—to help others heal as I have—would continue to unfold, and today I am still filled with awe and gratitude that this amazing journey of transformation came out of what once seemed like the worst thing that ever happened to me.

It never ceases to amaze me how a person's life can begin to transform, heal, and grow when we weave in the threads of hope and love. I am blessed and honored to serve others by providing energy balancing and guidance, which enables them to experience hope, courage, and strength as they discover life in a new way and their transformation begins.

Over the years, I've written reflections and poems that are precious to me and I lovingly share them with you. I hope they speak to your heart, allowing you to search deep within. I pray that you'll be blessed by them as they guide you toward your own life transformation.

My Prayer and Soul's Journey

Divine Father,

Empower me and assist me to lift Your children who have fallen,
shaking off the dirt and debris from their
wounded bodies, spirits, and souls.
Lord, may You guide and protect and lead me in the removal of
parasitic attachments that bind, bleed, drain them.
I invoke for Your divine Love to flow through me, for only Your
love can fill the holes of emptiness within them.
May each person's "inner child" receive the healing love and
light it has so yearned for since its inception.
Father, infill me with divine wisdom so that I may be used to
guide, teach, and grow each person You may send my way.
Assisting each person to stand, walk, and run throughout
their soul's journey in this physical world.
Quench the insatiable thirst of this world, may You be
received as water that resides within every cell
of our bodies and sustains our very life.
May Your divine spirit be poured out upon Your children
and may it fall upon us like rain so we may feel You.
May Your words be as food to grow our spiritual bodies
and let us learn to savor the aromatic beauty of Your presence
as You infuse into our lives.
Empower us, oh Lord, with divine wisdom, strength, power, and
freedom to soar like the birds and angels of the sky
as we seek whom we may assist through this life's journey.

Heavenly divine, You are our comforter, teacher, companion,
and lover of our very soul.
Yours is the only love that can fill every void;
You are the loving presence that infills, enfolds, and completes us.
For You are the divine...
the Universe that transcends us and connects us to all.

I AM the Witness

As I enter each life's story, it feels like I first enter their present time then, slowly, I'm sewn into their past. I'm there with them to witness a situation or trauma from a different or higher perspective view.

As the situation appears, I am guided how to erase the resonating frequencies and ripple effect of the trauma.

When I bring myself and the person forward into the present time, the trauma seems to resonate differently and is no longer affecting the present time. The client is now able to experience and live differently.

I experience the feeling of joy, love, and gratitude and sense a collective oneness within the Universe, all living beings, and elements on earth.

A feeling of completion and new beginning for the person.

I see and feel myself being guided and led by the divine love that connects us all while witnessing myself moving as a detective, counselor, warrior, messenger, and teacher on behalf of them.

Lord, may I be a channel of light, love, compassion, and healing on this earth, as You guide me, teach and lead me, as I passionately offer myself to this call.

On the day I wrote this reflection a terrible atrocity had occurred. I began to pray and intercede for love to pour into the hearts of every person and every being to awaken from their earth's slumber. We are all children of God and we are all of the one human race. Humanity, please awaken and ascend, shaking off what is broken to allow the suffering to come to an end.

Limited Reality

Believing in only what we can see,
now has created a limited mindset of reality.
We can't live within the projected holograms
which is shown, only to trust in the Great Unknown.

The world reflects man's relentless greed,
we don't need to suppress others to in order to succeed.
Fear of lack has come with great cost,
for I am afraid humanity's loss.
If we project fear more comes our way,
while blindly hoping for a better day.

Don't fearfully measure what life gives to you, give of your heart
freely and you will succeed too!
The fear of lack has created a delusion you see,
there is plenty enough for you and for me.
Earth's systems are crumbling into a great fall,
which is necessary for the ascension of one and all.
Frequencies that have held us so tight into this space,
will soon fall so we can love as one race.

As my personal transformation unfolded I began to realize that my previous need for material possessions could not fulfill the yearning desire deep within. This void can only be filled with a universal connection of light, love, and fire.

Transform Yourself ~ Search Deep Within

The quest fulfilling only earthly desires
quietly snuffs out the inner light of God's burning fires.

If we believe we must acquire it all,
we've set ourselves up for a great fall.
The lives which are built on shifting sand,
can quickly be erased by your own hand.

The foundations of life are invisible you see,
you must seek inward to find them,
it's only then that you can truly see.

Open your heart search deep within,
for this is when your life really begins.
The internal lessons of life that you'll see,
will enable you to love you and me.

I realized that holding on to the unforgiveness, anger, or rage from the accident only created energetic congestion, blocks, and tears within my body's energetic system, which led to greater emotional and physical dysfunction and pain. In choosing to forgive, however, I could release and dissolve these blocks, making space for physical and emotional transformation and growth.

Happy and Free

*A person's perspectives and one-sided view
can become critical condemning others, then you.*

*Another person filled with forgiveness, grace, and love,
knows the key to soaring way up above.*

*There is a secret to life for you and me,
of how to live in peace, love, and harmony.*

*Release oneself let it all go,
your foolish pride and your ego.*

*Rise above your circumstance, open your eyes don't you see!
You've chosen to believe in the anger, offense, and tragedy.
Release it all…you have a choice,
or pain will become your only voice!
You'll lose your life…It will pass you by,
because you've been so focused on the other guy.*

*Your mind has been stuck in this earths life's plane,
always seeing yourself a victim of tragedy and pain.*

*By releasing unforgiveness, hurts, and pain to God above,
you open yourself to receive healing and divine love.
This will ignite an enveloping flame
that releases and erases life's hurts, pain.
As you reflect on your life's journey,
You'll remember when you choose to live
peaceful, happy, and free.*

Trust in The Unknown

I don't fully understand, but what I know from my personal transformation is this...

In the hardest of times, when we are at our lowest, there is an opportunity for the greatest exponential growth and change of our lives.

If I had not suffered with depression, anxiety, panic, and a sense of complete helplessness, and feeling loss...I couldn't help people with this affliction.

If I had not been so severely physically injured for six debilitating years and lived with limited function...I couldn't help people with this affliction.

If my marriage was perfect, I would never have learned how to compromise, work through conflicts, sacrifice, and forgive...I couldn't teach couples how to release offense to grow and thrive.

I have no idea who I would be if I had not suffered beyond what I thought was my share.

This poem of faith came to me as I realized through those dark and lonely days I couldn't give up hope and let life pass me by.

Keep the Faith

No matter what you've been through, keep the faith.
It is never hopeless
no matter how many years have passed you by
waiting for your miracle.
Sometimes, the obstacle you think will destroy you
creates and opportunity for the greatest personal growth
in your life.

Realize that in our worst and darkest days,
a transformation may be in progress.

Divine Loving Light

There isn't an earthly language that can describe or explain
The touch of the divine loving light
as it releases life's hurts and pain.

This light can't be found by logic, reason for self-gain.
It transcends human conceptions
with our limited mindsets and brain.

Humanity is held bound by concepts and beliefs within their sight,
while starving and depriving their dying little light.

The Divine loving light
has no face, no body, boundaries, or walls,
It soars beyond world systems that are held so tight by us all.

A soul touched by the divine loving light
now begins to open its wings and soar,
dimensional spaces deep within and so much more.
This soul is now able to see the deeper connections
between you and me.

It is ancient, it is oneness, it is wisdom, this light,
but cannot be found by man's sight.

This consciousness is an enveloping flame,
And a soul touched by the Divine Loving Light
will never be the same.

Friend of Mine

Don't you worry friend of mine
Your healing journey is just in time

I'll stand by you night and day
You and I will make a way
For we are not of this world
But we are all light beings sent into the world
If everyone would let their light shine
Then their heart's would be as full as mine.

ABOUT THE AUTHOR: Darnell Florane Gouzy a Biofield practitioner holding certifications in several modalities, including, MCKS Certified Pranic Healer; and Neuro-Linguistic Programming. She is also a Transformation Specialist and AIS Stretch Therapist working in person and virtually with clients of all walks of life, including MLB, NBA, and NFL athletes. Darnell combines scientific and metaphysical principles to bring harmony within the mind and body to create sustainable life changes. Darnell contributed to the 2016 #1 bestseller *The Gifts of Grace and Gratitude*. In 2018 she lectured to the Louisiana Student Nurses Convention on *The Integration of Allopathic Medicine and Energy Medicine for Optimal Healing and Health*.

Darnell Florane Gouzy C.P.H., R.M.T., C.P.T.
Life Energy Therapies, LLC
darnellgouzy.com
facebook.com/LifeEnergyTherapies
Instagram/pranichealinglouisiana, Instagram/lifeenergytherapies

Me Becoming Me
Sue Urda

I am exactly the woman I want to be in this very moment, and yet I hold a higher vision of myself that I would have to make many changes in order to become. I would have to increase my patience and reduce my need for immediate gratification—this is tough for me because I pretty much want everything NOW. I must replace my somewhat lack mentality with an abundant mindset—been working on this one for years. My fear of standing out (i.e. being outstanding) must override my need to fit in and be well-liked. Trusting my gut, heart, and inner knowing—which I do way more now than I used to—would have to outweigh my thinking mind—which I like to rely on because I think I'm pretty darn smart. And perhaps most importantly, my self-acceptance quotient would have to increase dramatically so that my fear of being the me I am born to be is made manifest—this might be the biggest sticking point of all.

From the outside, most people would see me as an accomplished woman. In my twenties, I doubled my income in one year by being an assertive, fearless salesperson. I have enjoyed the freedom of being an entrepreneur for more than thirty years. Our companies have been on *Inc. Magazine's* list of the 500 Fastest Growing Private Companies in the U.S., twice. Our sign and display manufacturing business grew from $150k to $5 million in five short years. Our women's network improved the lives of thousands of women through connections in their business, personal, and spiritual lives. Through our publishing company, we have helped more than three hundred and fifty women become published authors—many of them as Amazon #1 Bestsellers. This is all great stuff that I know I should be proud of…and yet, I am definitely not where I want to be.

You see, even though this all looks good on paper, I know all of it could have been bigger, better, and certainly more fulfilling. We could have helped so many more individuals, employed more people, taught more people, and done even more great good in the world. And, we could have enjoyed greater financial success along the way too. But you see, over the years, I have been an exceptionally good underachiever AND I am an awesome procrastinator. And because I am not proud of these two traits—or perhaps I should call them habits—I have not allowed myself to be proud of the accomplishments either.

Transforming Sue

My life has been pretty much one transformation after another, and at this very moment, no matter when you're reading these words, I am in the midst of another one—yes, another transformation, right now. You see, I believe transformation is an ongoing process and that we experience birth, dying, and being reborn many times over in this lifetime, IF we're paying attention and IF we don't get stuck in the muck that inevitably shows up or take for granted all the good that comes our way. In my lifetime I have been presented, and sometimes bombarded, with amazing opportunities for growth, and each time I said yes or said no, took a step forward or back, or simply paused until the perfect timing presented itself, I set myself up for the next transformation.

I know my life has not been the same as anyone else's and I also know that we're more alike than we are different. Having said that, I have always used the lives and experiences of other people to expand my thinking and my awareness and allow myself to dream of what is possible for me.

In the late 80s my dad lost his executive VP job in NYC and had a one-year golden parachute. Because there was a certain amount of security in this, he set out to fulfill his dream of being his own boss and started a company. I admired his bravery and excitement so much that in 1989 I decided to join him in his dream, because, like him, I had decided I didn't want to have to answer to anyone else in my career. Little did I realize that when you own a business, there are still lots of people to answer to, like investors, clients, and vendors, accountants, attorneys, and bankers. Yes, there were many more choices available to us as the owners, nevertheless it sure was eye-opening. In 1994 my dad died suddenly and as the new head of the company I was left to deal with all these people I thought I would never have to answer to. Within a few short months, we were forced into bankruptcy, for the business and me personally, and I went through my first dark night of the soul.

For months, I was skittish, depressed, and filled with fear. I didn't know what to think or do, so I was running on autopilot. Many days, I hid in our basement (I called it "working from home"), because some of our old vendors were stopping by our new offices asking for me and still trying to get paid, even though the bankruptcy was final. For months, it felt like I was living a nightmare. No one knew all this except Kathy, my life and now business partner. To the outside world, it all looked pretty good—just a transition—because we started a new company in the same industry, leveraging the personal client relationships I had built. But looks can be deceiving, because inside I was hurting and living in fear.

I also was doing whatever I could to help my mom through the loss of her husband, my dad, which was tough because it took her a few years to come back to life and actually be present with us. She worked for us for a couple of years so she had something to do with her days, and I spent lots of time helping her prep the house for sale, making financial decisions, and mostly trying to soothe her pain. I did the best I could, but I was ill-equipped at the time. My thirty-four-year-old self had done only a small amount of personal development and spiritual growth work. I had been introduced by my dad to a few books by Wayne Dyer, Jim Rohn, and Zig Ziglar that had set me on a path of better understanding myself and the human psyche and motivation, but I felt out of my depth with both my mom and my business life. It took years, many business successes and failures, and lots of personal and spiritual work to get comfortable in my own skin and to more frequently call upon my innate knowing as my go-to for decisions.

Fourteen years later, in 2008, at a Journey workshop developed by Brandon Bays, I had a breakthrough around this upheaval...I mean, that transformative time in my life. During a breakout session in which we pictured ourselves around a campfire with someone we wanted to talk to, I found myself with my dad. He told me I did the right thing in how I handled the bankruptcy of the business, starting the new company, and how I was taking care of my mom. He told me he was proud of me, words I missed so much and apparently needed to hear. I remember feeling waves of his love washing over me and I broke down in huge sobs of both pain and relief. The pain because I missed his guidance and physical presence, and the relief because I felt for so long that I had been "holding my breath" and "waiting for the other shoe to drop" over those impossible decisions I had made. It was the first good cry I had had since his passing. In looking back, I realize that I was so caught up in all the "doing" for the business, my mom, and everyone else, and in being in survival mode for so many years, that I had not grieved the death of my father. That day provided an opening for me and helped me relax more into my path and myself.

Grief is a mysterious and personal journey, and there is no predictable timeframe or roadmap...only intense on and off emotions and finding a new normal that never feels quite satisfactory...until one day it does.

The death of my dad and then moving and settling into my own entrepreneurial life has been my most profound transformation... so far. Of course, every transformation, whether big ones like these or smaller ones are all significant and can be life-changing in their own way.

Looking back, I can see that the toughest part of that time in my life was that my dad wasn't there anymore. No more brainstorming with his brilliant big-picture thinking, no more cheerleader, no more wise words, no more shining light, no more big bear hugs. No more dad.

Becoming Me

As many women who struggle to show their real, unmasked self to the world, I've had to learn to get comfortable with and relax into being me. It's taken many years, and honestly, I don't know that I'm fully there yet. I imagine some women scratch their heads and don't know what I'm talking about and think "Well, of course you're you, who else could you be?"

On one hand, I think we choose to be whomever we want to be. I believe in unbridled possibility and I believe in self-destiny. On the other hand, I believe we are each born to our families and circumstances for a specific reason and come to this life with a divine purpose and innate gifts and talents to share. I believe it is our decisions and choices though that determine our destiny and the person we become.

I have decided to accept the many aspects who make up the me I am today while allowing for the creation or morphing of my personality to become the me of my ultimate vision. I am a woman in love with a woman with whom I have shared twenty-nine years so far. I am an entrepreneur who has started and closed companies, has been well-off and broke, thin and fat, healthy and unwell, a great friend and a total bitch. I can be laser-focused or all over the place, productive or procrastinate, creative or stagnant. I am a talker and an introvert, I like to speak to groups and I love intimate, heart-to-heart conversations, both about meaningful topics. I love that we are born into our first family and that we get to choose our friends who become the family of our life—and, if we're lucky, we choose our family as friends too.

A few years ago, I decided to stop coloring my hair. Within six months my dyed dark brown hair had grown out enough that I cut it super short to allow the silver to shine. I am grateful to be free from the chemical hair dye that I'm sure was messing with my autoimmunity. More importantly, this one act has freed me and given me more confidence to honor myself and allow that to shine through too. It was a difficult decision—until I made it. I don't think I'll ever color it again, but I know better than to say never (LOL).

Other transformative actions and decisions over the years include packing up our things and moving to Florida to a condo we found on the internet, sight unseen; releasing family relationships that didn't respect me and my life choices; and stepping more fully into my gifts as an intuitive and empath and more frequently using them with our clients. All these transformations made me stronger, kinder, more compassionate, open, and loving. They also let me know it was not only okay, it was absolutely safe and good to be me.

My current and most important years-long transformation, that has lived alongside and is woven into the many other transformations I've had, is me accepting me for me, and I am getting much better at it.

Although I still hear a fearful voice in my head from my childhood that says, *What will everybody think?*, it has become quieter and less insistent; and there's a louder yet gentler and more loving voice that says, *What do you think? How do you feel?* This new voice is now my saving grace and guiding light as I navigate my life and show up in the world as me.

ABOUT THE AUTHOR: Sue Urda is your *Feel Good Gal*. She has impacted thousands of individuals through her transformative talks and inspirational writings that teach people to embrace the power of feeling good. She is a two-time honoree on INC Magazine's list of the 500 Fastest-Growing Private Companies, and she is an award-winning and #1 bestselling author. As co-founder and Publisher of Powerful You Publishing, Sue has connected thousands of women for business, personal, and spiritual growth, and has helped more than 350 women achieve their dream of becoming a published author. Sue is passionate about helping people make meaningful decisions they feel good about and move them to actions that are aligned with their values. Sue loves assisting women to *'find the feel good' and live in that space every day.*

Sue Urda
sueurda.com
powerfulyoupublishing.com
facebook.com/sueurda
twitter.com/powerfulyou

Love Is an Action Word
Karen Flaherty

It was Saturday, June 23rd, at exactly 10 a.m. when my husband Jude and I said goodbye to the two little girls we had come to know and love so dearly as foster children over the past eleven months. I managed to hold it together as we hugged and kissed them and told them we'd always love them. But as soon as their car turned the corner I crumpled to the floor, exhausted and depleted from all the emotions I had bottled up over the past few months, including the uncertainty that we would ever see them again.

We had been locked in a battle with "H and G"'s previous foster parents for the right to adopt them. It had been brutal, with Family Court dates, mediation sessions, meetings with lawyers who gave us a one-percent chance of "winning" from the start, keeping the court papers that proved we were their "guardians" on us at all times, and, one weekend, even running from the other couple. Each day was an exercise in willpower I didn't know I possessed, putting one foot in front of the other and putting on a brave face in front of the girls. In the end, we made the King Solomon decision to drop the case and send H and G back to their previous foster parents so they wouldn't go back into "the system." It was the hardest thing we had ever had to do, and it was heart-wrenching.

No words were available to me—only the raw, inconsolable, defeated feeling of a mother who has lost her children and worries for their well-being. If they're not with us, will they be okay? Why would we be saying "I love you" as we let them go? Who does that? Will they be healthy and happy, will they thrive as they grow? Will we ever see them, hold them again? Would they adjust yet again when they went back to their previous foster parents for adoption? It had been a crucial year for H and G, who recently turned five and six years old, respectively. Their teachers thought they were doing great, had adjusted well and were healthy and happy. And so did we.

After a long while, Jude gently got me up and I crumpled into his arms as we both sobbed, neither able to console the other. As we talked and cried, we had to reassure ourselves that they would be okay. We had to. We couldn't imagine any other outcome.

And I knew in my heart they would be okay. H and G had lived with that family, which consisted of two parents and their four biological children, for over two years before coming to us, which was why they had "first right of refusal" in the adoption process. Though they loved H and G, they'd felt the girls, who are both developmentally delayed, needed more attention than they could provide. H and G came to us in August, but by the following May, the other foster parents had changed their mind and decided to move ahead with the adoption. It was a crushing blow, and we fought it with everything we had.

I also knew in my heart that it was H and G's choice to go back as well. For H, that foster mother was the only "mother" she remembered, since she'd arrived there at just fifteen months old. She had even called out for her "mother" while she was with us. It was a plaintive cry, a desperate cry, and I knew when I heard, "I want my mommy," that she wasn't referring to me. It took all the love and strength I had to comfort her during these times.

As for G, she loved the boisterous, fun, and loving environment of the other home. Yes, it was hectic and crazy at times, but she liked that too. G was happy in our home, but wanted to know if we could have a baby or two so she would have more siblings to play with. How do you tell a five-year-old that the reason we've decided to foster and adopt is because we *couldn't* have our own children?

Once upon a time, there was a girl who had learned plenty of life lessons, first from a rough childhood and then from lots of healing books, workshops and courses to figure out why things happened the way they did. At thirty-five, she met her soulmate in a co-ed beach house at the Jersey shore. They fell in love, got engaged on a trip to Ireland and two years after their meeting married in a beautiful church full of family and friends. Each was the oldest of six kids, but they settled on having three.

That "girl," of course, was me, and in my ideal fairytale once the husband arrived, the children would follow. Instead, our path would include years of miscarriages, lots of doctors and procedures, stress reduction methods, and all the latest alternative health methods. In our mid-forties we decided to give up on getting pregnant and instead focus on adoption. It would be several more years—I was around fifty—when we heard of two little girls who needed foster care. It was a miracle, and we took them into our lives, not really knowing a thing about parenting a four- and five-year-old, each with her own very particular tastes and opinions. We loved and laughed and grew with them for almost a year, until they left, taking our hearts with them. I literally thought I would die.

Later that awful day, more questions emerged. Questions like, What would become of us? What would we do now? How could we go on without H and G in our lives? Yesterday, we had been "parents," part of a school and neighborhood that loved us and H and G like family, making play dates and having and attending birthday parties. What were we now? How would we explain this crazy turn of events to everyone?

I was pretty inconsolable that summer. My family and friends called to check on me, but since I couldn't make it through a sentence about the girls without crying, we pretty much avoided talking about them. Instead, we talked about the weather and Jude's upcoming fiftieth birthday. I had decided to surprise him, under the guise of taking our families to dinner to thank them for all their support over the past year. Those gatherings had helped us both a lot.

Yes, things were looking pretty dark that summer, especially since it took weeks to pack up and ship the clothes, toys, and bikes that the girls had accumulated while living with us. Each piece of clothing, tenderly washed and folded, each toy part reassembled to look like a whole, each memory of when we last played with it, all took a toll. Even my therapist called the situation "impossible," at which point I probably should have left her but it didn't occur to me because she was echoing my own thoughts.

Finally, in August I received a lifeline when a dear friend told me about a "wise woman" she knew. It seemed like an answer to my prayers. During my appointment, the wise woman gently explained that what had happened to us was part of a soul contract that we had agreed to; more importantly, she told me that we would recover. Such a relief! I had never heard of a "soul contract" before, but what she said and the way she said it felt right and consoling and motherly. And she really seemed to understand what a traumatic event this had been for us. I wanted to believe her, and so I did.

Many lessons, she said, had come out of what we had experienced. Jude and I had learned to love unconditionally, and I had learned to love two little beings more than myself. It was a lesson I had needed to learn. Also, she said that I learned grace and patience as I lovingly took care of H, G, and my husband all that year.

She was right, of course. We'd learned so much about being parents, caregivers, and all the roles that come with taking care of two little people, which in years to come would allow me to be a better teacher and guide to my clients.

In addition to talking with this wise woman, I, along with my husband, researched ways to heal and feel better over time. We read a lot, and tried EFT (otherwise known as Tapping) and meditation, finding much relief from both. I finally found tremendous comfort and confirmation, as well as inner peace, when I came upon Human Design in January of 2009. My search for answers led me to hear Karen Curry speak at a Wellness Clinic in Princeton, New Jersey one snowy night. I listened as she spoke of her new book, *Inside the Body of God,* and at the end mentioned that she also ran Human Design charts on her website.

Human Design? I remember thinking. *I'll have to check that out.*

And I did, right away. I got the chart, had a session in March with Karen and started taking courses with her. I've been studying Human Design for eleven years now, and practicing for ten. It was the life-changing shot in the arm that I needed, allowing me to heal and grow and make the transformation from mother of two foster children to coach, helping many find their life's purpose and direction.

Fast forward to today: Jude and I now live in Florida, having followed our guts to warmer weather and less stressful lives. Since moving here, I'm feeling fulfilled and helping my clients by doing my Human Design work fulltime. I've also written a book about Human Design and teach it to mothers and other professional women, my intention being to spread this incredible modality to as many women as possible so that they understand how unique each child is.

So what was my transformation?

- Once I learned about Human Design, we kept listening to our guts, and not our heads. Now, if something feels right, we do it.
- We trusted that we would be taken care of, despite all the financial worries following the legal disputes.
- We learned to forgive ourselves for the missteps we thought we made with H and G.
- We kept our heads down and didn't get involved in discussions of what might have been.
- We realized that our temporary role as parents gave us so much compassion for all our friends and family who are parents and for all my clients. We humbly bow to their patience and endurance.
- We cherish our roles as aunt and uncle to twenty-four amazing nieces and nephews.
- We focused on all the good in our lives—our health, our

careers, our families.

- We were able to be there in mind and body when our mothers passed within months of each other, and one brother as well.
- And, finally, we took care of each other and remembered the good times with H and G, as we healed and now thrive.

We will always love H and G and have a special place in our hearts for them. We hold them dearly, with love, appreciation, and awe for what they gave us, what they brought us, and for what we've become because of them. Though losing them was agonizing, I now feel much wiser and more fulfilled, and able to be so much more compassionate and empathetic with my husband, friends and family, and clients. I'm also profoundly grateful for all these lessons, because if this story had ended differently, I wouldn't have the time or freedom to do what I do now with the passion, energy, and focus that I have. We learned that love is a verb and the only way to express it fully is to be in action for those you love.

ABOUT THE AUTHOR: Karen Flaherty is a certified Human Design Specialist and the best-selling author of *Getting to Know YOU.* Before finding Human Design in 2009, Karen spent thirty years in marketing, training, and sales positions in New York and New Jersey. She brings this wealth of knowledge of the corporate world, and her own life experience, to her Human Design coaching practice. Karen is passionate about helping her clients discover their purpose and their genius. She works with individuals, couples, and families, as well as businesses and entrepreneurs, to find a new way of reinventing their lives in the twenty-first century.

Karen Flaherty
Living by Human Design
livingbyhumandesign.com
instagram.com/livingbyhumandesign
amazon.com/author/karenflaherty

A Lesson in Forgiveness
Gina Reuillon, MSPT

For as long as I can remember I suffered from fear of rejection. I just didn't know what it was until I was about thirty years old and a counselor put a name to what I was feeling.

I grew up in an emotionally chaotic household, collecting memories that would carry a sting of pain well into adulthood. My parents were very young when they had me and my sister. My father, a professional musician, was mostly absent, and my mother suffered from depression. Their marriage was riddled with fights and heartache. I often hid away in a small cubby or closet in the home because I felt safe there. For some reason when in these small spaces I never felt alone.

As a result, I developed a fear of relationships at a very young age. To me close bonds equaled pain, so to keep the probability of that pain to a minimum I kept my circle of friends extremely small and all people at an arm's length. This fear stayed with me as I got older. I was very selective about who I let in and limited my "circle of trust" to two or three. There always seemed to be this dark entity looming around, ready to sabotage everything. I thought I had outsmarted the entity by erecting walls around myself and, indeed, for many years this formula seemed to serve me well.

In 2003, I started my own physical therapy practice. I hired a brilliant young assistant. Year after year she proved her worth and, in time, became one of my closest confidantes. I deeply appreciated her. I trusted her. Never in a million years did I expect her to betray me.

Well…never say never.

Four years after opening my practice, I attracted the absolute worst man for me which ended in a horrible divorce, my second. I was going through a very rough time and, due to the nature of the circumstances surrounding the divorce, had decided to work from home. I had three kids from my first marriage who were taking this hard and I wanted to devote as much attention to them as possible. During my absence, the culture at my office radically changed from one of love and servanthood to backstabbing and gossip. It got so bad that I fired the entire staff in one day—everyone, that is, except my trusted assistant. Now I know that sounds a bit crazy but it was what I was being guided to do at the time.

I had met the Lord on Lincoln Road in Miami on July 13, 1997. I was strongly considering divorcing my first husband and a friend asked me to accompany her to church before I made the final decision. I was met there by some really awesome people who cared for me and counseled me. After patiently allowing me to talk for two hours, the counselor finally asked, "Are you done?" He then listed three obvious mistakes I had made that led me to that place. "Now, it looks like you are making a mess of your life. Do you want to accept Jesus and see what He can do for you?" I immediately felt my heart melt and gave an emphatic YES. Truly that changed the course for me. I started studying the bible, praying, and making better decisions.

By the time I fired my staff I had been walking with the Lord for fifteen years. My certainty around the decision came from the guidance of the Holy Spirit, which over that time I had come to see as infallible. Still, the next few weeks were a little rough to say the least, but my trusted assistant was sticking by me as expected.

Then, to my surprise, the vibe between us suddenly eroded. She was quiet and aloof and an atmosphere of mistrust was birthed. When she handed me her resignation letter I was devastated, not only by the loss of an outstanding employee but the coldhearted manner in which she was leaving. I was deeply hurt. I felt deeply betrayed. I was shaken to the core.

How could this have happened? I thought, but I already had the answer. I had let her in. I had forgotten to apply my formula for preventing devastation.

I went home that day and sat on the living room chair, feeling just about every negative emotion—angry, scared, dejected, confused, and sad. I was heartbroken.

"This one hurts, Lord!" I cried as I looked up to Heaven. "I'm gonna need you to hash this out for me." I sat alone in my dark living room until I had the energy to drag myself to bed.

At two a.m. I was woken out of a dead sleep and felt a push to go back to my living room. I knew God had something to tell me.

I sat down in the same chair and said, out loud, "Okay I'm up. Please speak to me."

Immediately I heard, *Read 2 Samuel Chapter 11.*

This was a first for me. Sure, I had heard the small still voice and felt the inner promptings but never had I received such specific instructions. I knew the Bible pretty well but not well enough to know exactly what that scripture spoke of. Intrigued, I immediately grabbed my Bible and started reading. I had been sent to the famous chapter of King David falling for Bathsheba. The "cliff notes" go as such.

King David is walking in the palace and observes a beautiful woman bathing. He becomes inflamed with lust and decides he must have her. Although the woman, Bathsheba, is married, he cannot resist. He has her sent to the palace, lays with her, and she becomes pregnant. King David panics and calls for Uriah, her husband, and a general fighting in a war, to be pulled from battle and sent home. The first night the honorable general refuses to set foot in his own home and instead sleeps on the doorstep. When word gets back to King David, he escalates his plan. He summons Uriah for dinner and gets him drunk. King David is certain now Uriah's loyalty to his men will be diluted and he will sleep with Bathsheba and think the baby is his. His "Plan B" fails when Uriah refuses to enter his home again and King David goes to "Plan C," which is to have him murdered in battle.

That was how the chapter ended. More confused than ever, I closed the Bible, looked back up to Heaven and said, "Can you be a little more specific?"

Again the Holy Spirit spoke. "Gina, nowhere in My word do I tell you to trust people. I tell you to love them and *trust* Me. You see, that is how you are made. Human nature is such that when your backs are against the wall you are capable of doing almost anything to save your own skin. If that is how you are made then you should expect it can happen. When you follow My command to love people in spite of this you will never find yourself devastated again. You will look to Me as you trust Me to use all things in your life for good."

I was stunned. I was astounded. In that moment I was set free from the prison of fear of rejection. Having this understanding has allowed me to have relationships without walls, without unrealistic expectations and without fear. It's okay if I get let down now. I can release people in their human condition and overlook all offenses without feeling devastated.

This realization has transformed every aspect of my life, including the way I work. I'm convinced that at the root of most disease is a weakened immune system due to unforgiveness. While studying to be a physical therapist I was assigned the book *Love Medicine and Miracles* by Bernie S. Siegel, M.D. Dr. Siegel, an oncologist, was able to predict where he would find the patient's cancer (i.e. cervix, breast, et cetera) by interviewing them. He did this by specifically focusing on areas of the patient's life where guilt and unforgiveness were found.

I practiced traditional physical therapy for twenty years, and over the course of that time I began to observe patterns in my patients, patterns which indicated that dis-ease and chronic pain were strongly linked to their state of emotional and spiritual health. I am a true Type A overachiever and when I was not getting optimal outcomes for every patient I decided to add functional medicine to my training. Functional medicine looks at all body systems working together as a whole. These systems are set in a matrix of the following: Defense and Repair (immune response), Energy (metabolism/mitochondrial function), Biotransformation and Elimination (detox), Transport (cardio and lymph function), Communication (neuroscience communication), Structural Integrity (membranes and musculoskeletal integrity, and Assimilation (digestion/absorption). At the core of these systems is our spiritual state. If you can picture a tree with spiritual health as the trunk and systems of the body as the branches, you get a clear picture of the overall health of the patient. This allows me to look at all the body systems, not just the system of Structural Integrity, which is the primary focus of traditional physical therapy.

Unforgiveness causes the body great stress; in fact, it is cancer to spiritual health. This is probably why most religions place such strong emphasis on the subject. Proverbs 17:22 states, "A cheerful heart is good medicine but a crushed spirit dries up the bones." Our bone marrow is responsible for creating cartilage, bone, and fat, providing the basis for the immune system, and creating blood cells and platelets. That is quite a job for one area of the body. Unforgiveness causes bitterness. Bitterness is the opposite of a cheerful heart. What this passage is warning us is what we now know to be true in Functional Medicine—that the foundation of health stems from the spiritual condition.

Forgiveness takes practice, but it is life-giving and worth the effort. I've since learned strategies to quickly forgive people. I sit in a quiet place with my hand over my stomach and picture the face of the person who has offended me. I then intentionally flood love and forgiveness from my gut to the image of their face. I continue this until the thought of the offender causes me no pain. Then I know the process is complete.

Proverbs 4:23 says, "Guard your heart above all else, for it determines the course of your life." That's a pretty serious statement. The word heart in that sentence in Hebrew is *libbeka,* which means your inner man inside the body cavity. It is really referring to the system of

Assimilation (digestion and absorption). By practicing this exercise I can quickly transform the pain of all offenses into an outflow of love and forgiveness. Maintaining health in my spirit has improved my physical health. I do not take any prescription medications.

Maintaining a soul of forgiveness has also allowed my relationships to blossom. I no longer have fear of rejection and as a result I can be myself without conditions.

This has transformed my life.

ABOUT THE AUTHOR: Gina Reuillon was born with a soft spot for the "underdog." The desire to help others led her at the age of twelve to become a "candy striper" volunteer at a local hospital and, eventually, to a Master's in Physical Therapy. Except for a short stint on Wall Street, all of her jobs, including that of a mental health counsellor and an aerobics instructor, have involved helping people live better. For the past twenty-five years she has been in private practice as a physical therapist and in 2018 added Functional Medicine to her skillset. Gina remains committed to being part of the transformation of healthcare.

Gina Reuillon, MSPT
Ginareuillon@gmail.com
Ginasphysicalhealth.com
772-223-3440

The Darkness Creates Structure for the Light

Nora Yolles Young

D ark gives form to light. Without it and all of its shades of gray we would not have the infinite dimension of light that we see, sense, and experience. It is the unseen, nooks and crannies, behind-the-scenes infrastructure that supports the human reality, much the way the stagehands and production crew support a theater production. Our human drive to express ourselves, to be seen and shine "on stage," blinds us to the divine performance that encompasses all light and dark and in-between expressions. Without the dark shadows of life, the show would simply not go on.

Structures are planned and built in the dark. It is where our rest cycle, deep introspection, and so many of our healing processes happen. From the dark nights of the soul come our new and improved strategies for better living. The dark serves as the deep wellspring of wisdom that comes in the early morning hours. Yet as a collective, we are in a stage of growth and development where we reject the dark entirely as unnecessary, evil, and bad. We resist going to thoughts that dwell in dark places, lest we become entangled within it, sucked in, and pulled away from the perfection of the light. I include myself in this collection, for I too have spent a lifetime avoiding the darkness within myself.

Like our shadow when we walk in the sunlight, the shadow is ever present and dependent upon the expression of the light for its own expression. How I express my light effects the equal expression of my dark. They work in tandem, the low wave to the light's high wave.

Remember the old Tom and Jerry cartoons? We saw the silhouette of the scary monster; then, as the source of this sight was slowly revealed, we realized it's just a tiny mouse working with the light to create a frightening illusion. We laugh at the cartoon, but if we look closely we'll see its deeper meaning. What if everything villainous and frightening is at its heart a reflection of the drama we are creating in tandem with the light? And, if so, what are the implications of this perspective shift in our lives?

As Hermes Trismegistus famously said, "As above, so below, as within, so without, as the Universe, so the soul..." My journey has been one of discovering a more integrative and whole understanding of light and dark dynamics playing out within myself. As the above quote indicates, the inner dimensions also play out on a collective level. Part of my soul's work is to provide a loose context from which others can frame their understanding of true self—a self that includes all aspects: light, dark, and the entire spectrum of light frequency in between—as well as of the dimensions of light and dark.

What is the shadow self? For me, it's the part that feels bad and that I hide from others and sometimes even myself. It's the version of me I'm ashamed of, have pretended does not exist, or feel regret about having; the aspects of me that have done things I know were wrong. Like the time I accidentally hit a person's car while parallel parking during the early morning street-sweeping rush in San Francisco's Mission District. In a hasty and uncharacteristic move, I chose to leave the scene without taking responsibility for my mistake, something I've judged others for doing in the past. Most perplexing, perhaps, was the realization that I secretly enjoyed doing something so unlike me...so, well, bad. I don't tout this behavior, nor do I advocate it; however, it did inform me of a darker aspect of myself that needed to be acknowledged and held in a space of non-judgment and consideration.

Some may disagree, but I don't believe this to be a character or morality issue, but a nuanced matter that goes to the heart of the human condition. I see my clients as members of humanity as a whole, collectively wading through the mire of their inner shadows and demons.

This begs the question, how do we shift our perception about these shadow aspects? I can tell you what does not work, and that is judgment and shaming. If we deem an act as bad, something to be rejected, how can we truly understand the root of that act? I know that when I judge, shame, blame, or hide traumatic events, bad behavior or feelings of uncertainty, fear, pain, anger, panic, resentment, and victimhood, I splinter myself. I lose the opportunity to openly learn and grow from becoming familiar with that aspect. When I know my whole self, and the myriad of aspects that make up that whole, new possibilities and choices become available to me. I can then strategize in the light of self-transparency to become whatever I desire.

Healing my relationship with my inner darkness happened in 2011, when over a period of a few months I was shown two very dark past lives. Back then, I proudly referred to myself as a lightworker and light warrior. And, along with everyone else in the metaphysical community, I was filled with wide-eyed excitement about the coming end of the Mayan calendar on December 21, 2012. There was a feeling of awakening in the air. Something new was coming. What that was, no one really knew, except that it promised the demise of the dark evil doers. All the good people of the light would prevail to bring the next level of wisdom to humanity. Those who were ready would experience a physical and spiritual ascension into the lighter dimensions, leaving the dense dark behind forever.

I had developed an active meditation practice with the intention of opening my spiritual channels, increasing my intuition, and accessing my innate energetic healing abilities. One night, as I sat in bed for my usual ten- to fifteen-minute meditation, a sudden flash of a past life popped into focus. It was the 1950s and I was a very handsome man in my early forties, standing in the shadows of a huge sea barge. Behind me, someone had a pistol pointed at my head. I knew I was about to die, and I knew that I deserved it. You see, the me of this past life was a smart, calculated, and cold-blooded psychopath. I was a powerful player in the human trafficking trade, and the boat I was killed in was my very own human cargo carrier.

My eyes popped open and I came out of the meditation with a gasp. My shock had nothing to do with the fact that I had recalled a past life—I was training to become a regression hypnotherapist and had learned spontaneous recollections were quite common. Rather, it was because I was a bad guy, though, strangely, I felt no judgement of that previous self. I knew I'd had countless past lives, so why was I being shown that one, where I was bad to the core, cold, calculated, and driven by greed? I knew that as clearly as I know I am a good person in this life. How could that have been me?

A few months later, it happened again. While walking through the electronics section of Costco, I suddenly felt as if I were wearing long heavy black robes and a regal, shiny black headdress. I could physically feel the weight of them on my body. It was the oddest sensation to have the Costco reality and the past life reality playing out at the same time.

In an instant, I knew that I was a nearly eight-foot-tall, super muscular, almost god-like man with skin the color of mahogany and large, almond-shaped topaz eyes. I knew I was an incredibly powerful leader. There were no loving relationships in that life, just power, control, and doing whatever was necessary to stay on top. That is what fulfilled me. I later learned more about this life in a formal past life regression session. I was a ruler during what looked the age of the Aztecs, with complex building plazas and ziggurat-like pyramids, though I cannot be certain that it was located on planet Earth. And I did some unspeakable things in an effort to satiate my hunger for power. I had people brought to me to be sacrificed, then harvested and consumed their pineal glands as a type of power booster to my system. Now, as I became aware of my brutality, I sobbed in cathartic release. It felt so horrific, yet I knew it to be true.

Like many of my clients, I had romanticized my past lives and assumed that if I ever had a regression I would be shown incarnations filled with glory, fame, and prestige. That is rarely the case, however.

As the purpose of regressions is to inform us so we can gain access to broader perspectives and enhance our current life experience, more often than not, the lifetimes we see are "average," with poignant or instructive memories that may even include our own brutal, violent, or evil acts. What was the point, I wondered, of knowing that my soul had been so dark?

In 2014, while training to become a Life Between Lives therapist, I had the opportunity to find out more about my soul's journey. Developed by Dr. Michael Newton, this type of spiritual regression takes clients to the place their souls reside when they're not in physical form. Newton found that we all have a council of elders that advises and supports us as our infinite souls evolve. During my session I was able to visit with my counsel, who shed some light on my development over many lifetimes. These beings had a sense of humor and even laughed as they told me that my soul has been very slow to evolve. They mentioned that I had taken a long and difficult path to get to my current stage of evolution, and jokingly referred to my need to explore every avenue, including the dark ones, over thousands of lifetimes as "leaving no stone left unturned."

As mentioned earlier, I also came into my work as a healer and hypnotherapist with grand notions of being a bright beacon of light for all. I had clearly identified the light as the side that I am in service to, and rejected the dark parts of myself as something bad, something to be feared, something totally external to me, and something to be defeated like the dark empire that has poisoned the hearts and minds of humanity.

Though I was familiar with the idea of the Universe being in harmony with all frequencies of the light spectrum, I had the same blind spot as many powerful healers with regard to the true purpose and function of the darker aspects and dimensions of life and reality. It wasn't until those dark past life memories, and my training as a transpersonal hypnotherapist, that I started to gain access to what my soul wanted to know about my relationship with the dark.

And what of the truly dark and evil stuff that happens in the world, the violence against and oppression of innocents? That's got to be something to reject and fight against, right? Something we can point a finger at and separate ourselves from and call out as injustice? Yes, but when we do so without deeper introspection we might be missing a massive opportunity to learn more about ourselves.

We each struggle with honoring the push and pull taking place within, just as the world is always seeking balance between Ying and Yang. This is our process of transformation, both individually and collectively and taking place over countless incarnations. Collectively, we are still in a phase of victimhood, where personal responsibility is abdicated for blame. That is not a good or bad, right or wrong thing, but simply a phase of maturity that we will eventually move past as we shift to a higher perspective. No human will evolve before their time. When evolution happens is entirely up to us.

ABOUT THE AUTHOR: Nora Yolles Young C.Ht, C.I., LBL® holds a Bachelor of Arts in Human Origins and Prehistory from The University of Redlands, Johnston Center. Nora considers her work as a certified integrative and regression hypnotherapist and instructor; Life Between Lives® therapist; consciousness coach; and healer to be both her art and her soul's purpose. In her twenties Nora worked as a contract archaeologist in Hawaii and California; today, she blends her understanding of consciousness and people and cultures throughout the ages with innovative healing tools in her one-on-one and group sessions, trainings, lectures and publications. Born and raised in Hawaii, Nora now lives with her husband and two children in central North Carolina.

Nora Yolles Young
Nora Young Hypnotherapy
NoraYollesYoung.com
Info.younghypno@gmail.com
808-224-4864

Role Reversal
Kathy Fyler

I t was a beautiful April afternoon in sunny Southwest Florida and I was getting ready to have a relaxing dinner when the phone rang. It was my dad.

"Kath," he said calmly, "your mom fell. Her leg hurts. I think it's not too bad. Can you come over?"

"Sure, I'll be right there." I thought from the tone of his voice that Mom had probably walked into the dishwasher door again because she forgot it was open and most likely got another pretty good gash on her leg…something she had been doing with more frequency lately.

I live about ten minutes from my parents' house, and lately I think the car can get there all by itself. That day I ran into a bit of traffic, which in Naples means it takes an extra couple of minutes to get through a busy intersection. My dad was waiting for me at the door.

"Did you not leave right away?" he said, sounding a bit frazzled.

As I entered the kitchen, there was Mom on the floor. She had her head down and wouldn't move. She was complaining of pain in her left hip. I assessed her leg and hip and it didn't seem like anything major was wrong. My dad and I tried to get her up, but it was more of a struggle than we expected (she can't weigh more than a hundred pounds), but she cried in pain and became very dizzy. So, we put some pillows on the floor and laid her down again and called 911. The ambulance came and took her to the hospital. Mom had broken her hip and needed surgery.

After the Fall

Mom was "officially" diagnosed with Alzheimer's the year before, in 2018, but there had been many signs over the years that her cognitive ability was declining. Up until then, she was very good at "hiding" the symptoms and my dad was in denial. Who wants to believe they are losing their partner in life? But it became harder and harder to ignore what was going on and after a couple of disturbing events witnessed by others, I realized that my role with my parents was changing. My dad had turned eighty-two and Mom, seventy-nine. When they came due for their annual checkups, I asked if I could tag along, my goal being to get a referral for a neurological evaluation for my mom.

I'll have to admit, that it was a bit out of my comfort zone to ask (or more accurately, tell) my parents that I'd like to be part of their assessment. I had been a nurse many years ago, so I levied that to my advantage to get them to agree. I wanted them to be independent, but I knew that I needed to make sure we got help for Mom and confirm that she should no longer be driving.

Things had been heading in this direction since 2012, when Sue, my life partner of nearly thirty years, and I moved to Florida. We had traveled to the beaches of Southwest Florida for our network's tour events in 2010 and loved the weather and the energy. We also knew that my parents would end up here and that we'd be closer to them. They were getting older and our business allowed us to work from home and be flexible, so I was in a great position to enjoy and help them through their sunset years.

My dad has always been the typical traditional head of the household and we never questioned his decisions—after all, he was "the dad." As he was aging, though, it became clear that not all decisions he made were made based on his current age and situation. For instance, in 2017, Hurricane Irma was forecasted to plow right through Naples as a Category 4 or 5 storm. I tried to explain to him that staying in their home with Mom was not a good idea. Several of their friends were "hunkering down" to ride it out, and he wanted to do the same. This was the first time I felt like my role was changing.

We had three days to get out of town and there was a lot of push and pull. I raised my voice and "fought" with him, something I had never done before. It was really tough for me to stand up to him, but their safety came first. Thank goodness we left and stayed in a hotel/casino in Mississippi for ten days, because Irma devastated the town and left us without power for fifteen days. Being home would have been a nightmare for Mom because by that time any type of change made her very angry and caused a huge personality shift and confusion for weeks to follow.

The Toll of the Caregiver

After the diagnosis, I attended some support groups at the local Alzheimer's organization. The local chapter was very active and the people who run it were extremely caring and helpful. They had support groups and classes on all aspects of Alzheimer's. One of the most striking things I learned is that seventy percent of all caregivers die before the person with the disease, so there was a great deal of emphasis on the importance of self-care.

The months after Mom broke her hip, were extremely difficult for my dad, myself, Sue, and my brother and his partner. Mom did a stint in the hospital and rehab facility and came home about six weeks after the fall, and even then someone had to be with her 24/7 for the next few months. With the nature of the disease, any disruption, change, or illness can lead to progression of more rapid cognitive decline, and this is what happened with Mom. I am not sure which was tougher, helping Mom with the tasks of daily living or the emotions associated with witnessing her mental decline. I knew it took a huge physical and emotional toll on Dad, as he would not spend a night away from her. Trying to get my father to take care of himself…well, let's just say it wasn't in his nature and I was concerned about him as well.

Dad has always been very healthy, and at eighty-three he was proud that he took no medications. He was active, played golf two to three times a week, and worked outside in the garden. But now, just two weeks after Mom returned home, dad had a dizzy spell and called me to come over. He seemed okay, but a couple of days later he still didn't seem quite right, so we took him to the ER as recommended by his general practitioner. They found that his blood count was extremely low and he was hospitalized for internal bleeding. This was the start to an almost year-long journey of doctors and hospitalizations.

Once my dad's health stabilized, it felt like we settled into a more normal routine.

Sue was feeling a little off and thought maybe her blood sugar might be low, so we bought a glucose meter. Her levels were fine. Come to find out, mine were not! What the heck? The stress of the whole situation was taking a toll on me too. I guess if you think about it, I had the risk factors—love of all things sugar, weight in the belly, a strong family history of type II diabetes, and inactivity due to our blossoming business and spending lots of time with Mom and Dad. I was not ready for this and thought, *What am I going to do?*

First, I had to deal with the emotions of the family situation, and wow, there were a lot of emotions. There was the loss of the mother that I knew. There was sadness for my father, because he was losing his relationship with his wife and partner of over sixty years. There was the incredible amount of patience and energy it took to be present when they needed me. There was also anger because the situation seemed daunting and was a big change to my life.

Without the support and love of Sue, I am not sure how I could have done it. She was always the one who was there for me, helped me to calm down when I was angry, helped me to see when I needed to be compassionate or strong, and helped me prepare for countless tough conversations.

Caring for the Caregiver – I Guess that's Me

In the midst of all of this, I had to make a major lifestyle change for my health. I had been doing a keto diet on and off since 2017, but totally threw it out the window after my mom broke her hip. A keto diet is basically a low-carbohydrate, high-fat diet that is good for cognition and clarity, weight loss, and reducing inflammation. Now, it was time to get serious. Afterall, with my mom's Alzheimer's diagnosis, which many doctors refer to as "Type III Diabetes," it was now even important for me to protect my brain and cognition. In November of 2019, after some very scary blood glucose readings, I gave up my carbs, started intermittent fasting, and started walking a few miles every day.

The walking helped with physical movement and, perhaps more important, gave me time to be with my thoughts. When there was a lot of busy-ness, there was no stopping and taking stock of where I was emotionally. The walking helped me think through and release some of the stored-up emotions.

I am happy to say that my blood sugar levels are now under control and I continue to adjust to a life without my beloved sugar. I know that taking care of myself is important so I can also take care of Mom and Dad.

Communication Transformation

My family has never been good at communicating. My whole life we avoided all controversial topics and never discussed anything personal, emotional, or sensitive. Like when I opened up and talked to my parents about my ten-plus-year relationship with Sue and my mom said, "Oh yeah, we know. We thought you didn't want to talk about it." Meaning, *they* didn't want to talk about it. These days, there are plenty of opportunities for me to become a better communicator. I've had many tough conversations with my dad and my brother—who also lives in SWFL. This is a new experience for me, and I am doing my best to embrace it as a chance to grow.

Over the last couple of years, I've been reminded of this communication and understanding gap. There was the time we were preparing for Mom to come home from rehab. Dad, Sue, and I went to all the meetings with the social workers, nurses, and physical therapists. There were recommendations of how to prepare the house for Mom's safety. This was especially important because her short-term memory was very limited and she couldn't follow instructions day-to-day. Sue and I prepared the house by moving furniture to provide adequate space, taking up throw rugs, and putting up handrails. Mom and Dad came home and within a day, most of the safety measures were reversed! Clearly, Dad's denial was still alive and kicking. I remember him saying to me, "Thanks, Kath, for all you do, even if I don't agree." *Wow,* I thought, *this is going to be tougher than I expected!*

My goal with my parents is for them to live independently for as long as they can, enjoy themselves to the fullest and, most importantly, stay safe. This means navigating the nuances and balancing my need to compel them to do things that I think are good for them with their need to make their own decisions and feel like they haven't lost control. Most days they have cereal for breakfast, peanut butter and jelly sandwiches for lunch, and always a Klondike bar for dessert (sometimes both lunch and dinner). Sure, I'd love for them to have a salad and go lighter on the sugars to keep further mental decline at bay, but I've learned that I just have to let some things go.

Most days, I am feeling my way through this crazy and wild dance with fluidity and flexibility. I am learning to let my intuition and knowing guide me with decisions and interactions with my parents. At fifty-nine years of age, one would think that I've done all the "transforming" I need to do, but that's not how life works. This journey has taught me a lot about myself and I have grown through the highs and lows, trials and tribulations, and the many growth opportunities that seem never-ending. Through it, I've learned to be a great "parent" to my parents; most importantly, I've come to recognize than I am more capable that I thought possible.

ABOUT THE AUTHOR: Kathy's earlier career includes being a Critical Care Nurse, Project Manager for a technology firm, owner of a $5 million manufacturing company, and Co-Founder of a national Women's Networking company. In 2005, she followed her calling to make "more of a contribution to what matters most in this world". Using her experience and passion for technology, reading, and people, she co-founded Powerful You! Publishing to fulfill her personal mission of assisting women to be authentic and share themselves broadly online and through the published word. Kathy is a Publisher, Amazon #1 Bestselling Author, and tech enthusiast who loves the beach, sports, and travel.

Kathy Fyler
Powerful You! Publishing
powerfulyou.com
facebook.com/kathyfyler

Undoing the Doing
Renée M. Dineen

It was 2014, and I was coming up on my twentieth year in demanding roles in global organizations. I was grateful for my work. Passionate about my work. I was also so exhausted and so weary that my bones ached most days. I was moving from one thing to the next with no time to process, reflect, or celebrate. I was running at an unsustainable pace, and my body and relationships were paying for it.

My heart knew it was time to make a change—to leave my corporate life and launch a boutique coaching and consulting practice that focused on doing the deeper work required for lasting personal and professional change. I also knew I needed to rebalance my life—change the energy and flow of my day-to-day choices so I could be more present with my loved ones.

Yet the louder voice in my head kept telling me I had to stay—and to stay quiet. And so the tension built, igniting a crisis between my head and my heart.

Following My Heart, Finally

I had been back in the US about a year after living and working oversees for five when that quieter voice, the one telling me it really was time to leave, turned up the volume.

"Who you are," she said, "What you have done, and what you have—is already enough."

Enough?

Couldn't be. Yet my heart leapt at the chance it was true.

Thus began my journey to leave my corporate life—the people, contexts, and identities that served and fueled my entire professional career. I knew I would grieve and I did. I also believed that what would be birthed would make the grief worth it.

However, I made one very naive assumption, which would take me on a much bigger journey. With so much white space now available on my calendar, I thought I would organically transform to fit that new life. I thought I would very simply stop pushing, driving, doing, and improving. That is definitely not what happened.

My Addiction

In addition to being a coach and consultant, a wife, and a mother, I am also an addict. An action junky, who regularly sacrifices her "way of being" for the reliable high of "doing." And like, any addict, owning my addiction was the first real step towards recovery.

For most of my life I'd convinced myself I had it pretty well together. I had a strong marriage, two great kids, enriching and fun friendships, and a fulfilling career.

Yet, many days I still felt empty. Feeling that who I was, what I had, and what I had done, was not yet enough. So, I chased more. I did more. But more did not settle my soul, fill my heart, or strengthen my relationships.

I remember the first time I saw myself in my addiction. It was 2014, and one morning while eating breakfast my spoon started clattering against my cereal bowl. I had developed a tremor in my hand. A few days later, I started speaking with a stutter.

I called my doctor, who announced that my gender and age bracket put me in the "high risk patient profile" for multiple sclerosis and she was scheduling an MRI.

Thankfully, it was not MS…it was stress. I had been working crazy hours which included traveling and getting way too little sleep. On most days, I found it difficult to breathe—to take that full deep breath that resets your nervous system when you need it most. I also felt trapped by my drive to keep "doing" and yet helpless to change it.

The possibility of having a life-changing disease was a wake-up call. It was time for me to face my addiction and acknowledge the negative impact all my years of "doing" was having on my health and my relationships.

This required me to shift my belief structure about what it looked like to contribute—to be seen and acknowledged not just for what I did but for who I was. This may be easy for some; for me it was anything but.

The Real Work Begins

It was January 2017, about fifteen months since I left my executive role in biotech to give myself a shot at doing work that would fill my soul and sustain me, within my new framework. My progress had been slow. On most days, I was still chasing that reliable high I got from my "doing life."

The breakthrough came at a women's retreat I attended with my daughter. During the closing session, women were being invited to share the impact the weekend could have on their lives. As others spoke, I could see my daughter prodding me with her eyes. She wanted me to be the mom she knew, the one who does without exception. But in this moment, I heard a wiser and more authentic voice inside of me, saying, "Stay put, sit, observe, receive."

A few seconds later, a more familiar voice came onto the scene. "Why are you here if you don't step into the circle? Who are you if you're not contributing?" I listened to the two voices within me battling it out and eventually had to leave the room. It may not seem like a very significant moment but somehow I knew it was.

As I looked out at the ocean I reflected on just how many times this battle had played out in my life. How many times this drive to do, to contribute, to effort had ruled me. And, how few times I had given myself permission to honor that small but important moment we are almost always given before taking an action, to pause and decide. Then I thought about all the things I had done that weren't authentic because they did not come from a place of deeper knowing that they were what I needed or wanted.

My decision to not step into the circle that morning honored that quieter, long-ignored voice within me that said, "You don't 'have' to do this." And that one small win gave me hope that I could actually practice this in my life more regularly. And what if one of the choices I could make for myself was to do nothing—to take "Authentic Inaction," two words that came into my consciousness that morning.

What Fueled My Addiction

I wish I could say that from that moment, I had learned what I needed to learn and my life finally and magically changed. It didn't.

For the majority of my life, I had been proud of being a doer. In fact I came from a long line of doers. My grandmother was, my mother is, and, thanks to my example, my thirteen-year old daughter was as well.

Yet, this wasn't just a family trait, but one prevalent in most, if not all of the contexts I lived in. To let go of my bias towards action would require a dismantling of a systemic bias in a world I am part of and helped to create. Being a doer is not only accepted—it is honored, encouraged, and expected. It's an identity, rooted in our culture. What we do has become synonymous with who we are.

The truth is, many suffer from this crippling addiction, to the tune of billions of dollars a year in health care costs, corporate burn-out, and wasted effort. It has contributed to broken relationships and a loss of our truest sense of who we are in the world.

Transformation Was Finally Possible

My own three crucible moments—my tremor, leaving my corporate life, and not stepping into the women's circle that morning—finally convinced me I could heal from my addiction.

While I can still easily be drawn into my need to "do," I've stayed on my path, exploring this concept I've named Authentic Inaction™.

I've also curiously but painfully witnessed the action junkies all around me. Why did they choose to "do," often at the expense of "being?" What was their addiction about?

Here are 5 DOERS I've identified and come to know…and in some ways, find myself in each of them.

The Achieving Doer: They do to be recognized, and build-up their sense of self. They have most likely been acknowledged for their ability to get things done so this is directly connected to their self-worth.

The Avoiding Doer: They do to avoid being confronted with the bigger questions and challenges in life. As they keep themselves occupied with tasks, the more important issues do not get addressed.

The Controlling Doer: They do because they want it done and are often not willing to wait for someone else to do it. This makes them feel more in control, but this can push others away, leaving them feeling alone and unsupported.

The Perfecting Doer: They do because they think no one else can do it as well as them. Their standards often result in over-engineering and over-efforting and yet, no matter how well things are done, it still never quite feels good enough.

The Supporting Doer: They do for others, and are really good at it. Doing makes them feel needed but also obligated, and when they do too much without asking for anything in return, they end up feeling unappreciated and resentful.

In working with my clients I have found that while all DOERS share commitments, deadlines, events, and projects we authentically want to do—others we believe we have to do—we still have the freedom to choose whether we have our doing life…or it has us.

Having identified the five DOERS and how they show up in my experience, I created four steps to apply Authentic Inaction™ into my life. I also teach and use these steps with my coaching clients.

Step 1 is simply about being aware.

This is the moment when we look at ourselves in the mirror and say, "I am an action junky." Without first becoming aware of the addiction and how it is playing out in our lives, we are powerless to change it.

Step 2 is adoption of some new beliefs.

The first belief is that our addiction to "doing" is not emotionally and physically healthy. It is not serving us or those who love us.

The second belief is around authenticity—which is not just about knowing who we are, but understanding how, more than anything else, our actions reflect to others who we are.

The third belief is a rejection of the lie that says, "Do more, it is not yet enough."

Step 3 of 4 is sitting with the question, "Who am I and therefore, what am I to do?"

Start simply, by making a list about what inspires you, what depletes you, what slowly sucks the soul out of your body. Look for themes; the obvious; the outliers.

Do you host a holiday dinner every year but don't enjoy it?

Do you raise your hand to take on a project you don't really want to do or even have time for?

Do you commit to waking up early to meet a friend for a workout knowing what you truly want and need is to sleep in?

When our own patterns and reasons for doing become clear, and we are fully committed to connecting who we are with what we do, we will make the right choice the next time a yes or no, do-or-not-do moment arises.

And the final step, Step 4, is being willing to fall and choose again.

We need to accept that in many circumstances we won't hear, or even listen to, our more authentic voice. When we fall into that familiar pattern of saying yes when we mean no, we need to pause and take a deep breath. Be willing to sit with the discomfort that comes when we are at risk yet again, of taking another action that does not line up with who we really are. And next time, choose again.

Summary

Being an action junky is an addiction, and like other addictions, recovery is possible. When we begin to undo the doing in our own do-crazy worlds, we'll begin living a healthier and more authentic life.

My hope in my own life, is to stay committed to my own recovery. To wholeheartedly believe that who I am, what I have, and what I have done is already enough.

My hope for all of you who resonate with this addiction, is to feel inspired and equipped to take your own first step with Authentic Inaction™.

ABOUT THE AUTHOR: Renée Dineen is an international thought leader playing at the intersection of business, psychology, and well-being. In 2015, this self-described recovering work-a-holic and "doing" addict left her executive role in biotech to do work that mattered to her without sacrificing the other parts of her life. Today, her consulting firm inspires leaders and teams to develop while retaining their authenticity in the face of challenge. Renée has been featured on podcasts, presented on global stages, and published dozens of articles on leadership and personal growth. Her 2020 Ted Talk, Authentic Inaction™, in which she demystifies our culture's obsession with busyness and doing, reached over 500k views. Renée lives in California with her husband and two children.

Renée M. Dineen
RMD Coaching & Consulting
reneedineen.com authenticinaction.com
reneedineen@gmail.com
650-452-0185

Defying the Odds
Sanae Okada

"The part can never be well unless the whole is well." ~Plato

I was paralyzed with fear when I was first diagnosed with stage four "incurable" cancer. I was essentially given a death sentence that day, a sentence that has long since expired. In the pages that follow, I'll share a bit of my story with you, a transformative journey that led not to my becoming a cancer survivor, but a cancer thriver.

In May of 2013, I was going out of town with a friend to enjoy some time off over the long weekend. I had gone for a laser hair removal session so to be nice and smooth in case we went into a pool or hot tub during our trip. During my appointment, the laser therapist worked around my hairline, underarms, and bikini area, all of which are close to lymph nodes. I remembered this session was more painful than usual and my body felt extremely sensitive. Afterward, I noticed for the first time my lymph nodes looked swollen and felt firm to the touch.

After a few weeks went by and my lymph nodes still appeared puffy, I went to see my family doctor to get it checked out. She had me monitor it, and after another month I was sent to get an ultrasound at the hospital. To my surprise, the technician stated that the lymph nodes in my neck and upper chest area were enlarged and they felt it necessary to send me for a groin biopsy. At this point, I was still not very concerned since I felt healthy and was enjoying an active and fun summer.

In early fall, my first biopsy appointment arrived. In the interim I had started getting a few other symptoms in addition to the enlarged lymph lodes—things like little welts on the tops of my feet that were incredibly itchy, worse than the worst mosquito bite. I also noticed that my skin appeared a bit thinner and scratched and bled easily. These symptoms were relatively mild, but sudden and strange, and made me feel like something might really be wrong. Over the next month, I began feeling fraught with anxiety and fear about the potential gravity of my situation.

After my surgical biopsy, I went to the surgeon's office to hear my results. I remember wanting to be dressed well and have my makeup and hair done nicely for this official news. Oddly enough, it did not occur to me to bring another person to my appointment as a witness or for support. In retrospect I wish I had, but at the time I still didn't realize how significant this appointment was. Or maybe I was just in denial. Probably a bit of both, which is why just a few minutes later I found myself in complete and utter shock.

As soon as I heard the words "follicular lymphoma," it was as if the world had stopped. He went on to explain that this was a cancer of the lymphatic system and classified as a "blood cancer," but at the time I could not hear any of it.

All I could think was, I don't understand. How could this have happened? I thought I was a vital thirty-something woman who lived a very healthy and active lifestyle. I was even considered "the healthy one" or "health nut" among my friends. I don't remember leaving the appointment, but I do recall it was raining very hard as I walked to my car. It was one of those gloomy fall Vancouver days and the perfect backdrop to my dramatic news and feelings of dread.

The whole experience was surreal. At first, I was stunned and walking around in a haze like I was mourning. I would play out my funeral in my mind, visualizing how it would look and organizing it like it was a party or event. For weeks, I did this almost daily, usually while driving home with tears streaming down my face. I think I needed to do this to come to terms with my own mortality and grieve my old self.

Around the same time, I had a whirlwind of appointments related to my cancer diagnosis. It all happened so fast that I barely had a chance to digest what was happening to me. In my first appointment with my oncologist and her team, I was given the strong recommendation to undergo a type of chemotherapy.

Everything in my body screamed against this choice. I had lived most of my life naturally so I was very apprehensive of putting pharmaceutical drugs in my body. However, when faced with the scary diagnosis of stage four cancer, my fear took over and I put my health in the hands of the doctors. They were adamant, and at the time I did not have enough knowledge or conviction to go against their advice. So, I reluctantly scheduled my first chemo treatment after the holidays.

After a month of riding a roller coaster of emotions from fear to grief, sadness, and hopelessness, I started to accept my situation. My optimistic nature and entrepreneurial spirit kicked in, and I flipped the script to focus on what I needed to do to be proactive and positively impact my situation. Looking back, I realize I approached my health and cancer diagnosis like any new venture. I just made a commitment to myself that I would do whatever was in my power to heal from this disease, and off I went.

On January 17th, I had my first infusion of the chemotherapy. My dear friend Irene, who had survived breast cancer years earlier, took me to the hospital and was a great support. I was nervous and did not know how I would feel, but to my surprise the physical discomfort was not as bad as I had anticipated. It was the following week, after my second chemo appointment, that things started to go south. I ended up in the Emergency a couple of times over the next several days because I was hot and had major nausea and sickness. On my second visit, I was admitted to the hospital with a dangerously high fever of 40C (104F). My body was also swollen and breaking out into large reddish welts. It was absolutely terrifying. Various ER doctors and nurses came to check on me, including a team of oncologists from the Cancer Agency.

Later, I was moved to the Intensive Care Unit (ICU). The room was dark, stuffy, and had a heavy energy as the patients were unconscious and hooked up to life support machines. Little did I know at the time, I too was fighting for my life.

When my homeopath Sharon learned that I was in the ICU and likely going to be there for a while, she galvanized our Jikiden Reiki® community. Jikiden Reiki is a form of energy healing that is a physical treatment but can also be sent remotely from any location to the recipient. After a few days and many Jikiden Reiki treatments from various practitioners, my fever started to go down and my condition was stabilized.

I was still very ill but was transferred to another ICU room which seemed less critical. My mother came daily and helped feed me as I lost ten pounds while at the hospital. The doctors and especially the nurses in the ICU were amazing and made me feel safe during such a harrowing time. I was very grateful for their assistance and for the help of my healing community, family, and friends.

After what I call the "chemo attack," I decided to listen to my body and completely stop my medical treatment. Instead, I chose to do 100% holistic treatment for cancer, which was more aligned with my beliefs and training as a holistic practitioner.

My body had given me a clear and strong message that doing chemotherapy was not for me and could possibly kill me. As it was, it had caused major side effects like intense joint pain, nausea, and extreme fatigue that would last for months; it also demolished my white blood cells so my immune system was very low. I remember when I got home, I barely recognized my face due to my weight loss and sunken eyes. The toxins in the chemo had completely depleted my life force.

For the next year, I adhered to a comprehensive holistic program under the guidance of my homeopath and holistic team to essentially detox my body from the chemo and treat the cancer. My protocol included daily homeopathic remedies and acupuncture, visceral physiotherapy, chiropractic work, and regular Jikiden Reiki treatments. These therapies worked to gently drain toxins out of the body and supported my immune system so I could start healing properly.

I always felt much better after I received treatment, experiencing less pain and nausea and feeling more energized and clear-minded. It was so healing and improved the quality of my life significantly. It was like a part-time job to keep up with the daily holistic regime of remedies, treatments, juicing, and a strict healthy diet but it all worked to bring me back to health and treat the cancer naturally.

As part of this holistic approach, I also put myself in a "spiritual bootcamp." This encompassed intensive work on the psychological and spiritual levels to help release any past traumas or negative beliefs that we all carry from the past and keep in our subconscious mind. I understood that in order to fully heal I had to heal my mind, which meant leaving no stone unturned. It was arduous, exhausting, emotional, and very difficult at times, but also well worth the effort.

I now realize that my cancer diagnosis was the result of a "perfect storm." In the months preceding my diagnosis, I was in a state of complete grief and loss after separating from a best friend of twenty-six years due to her alcohol addiction. I was highly stressed for an extended period of time as I worried for her and her children and tried to accept the fact that nothing I did would stop them from going down this dark path. We all have a tipping point and for me, that was it.

I came out on the other side of this journey with a new perspective on life. I became more focused on what mattered and more grateful for the small things. Some things I used to care about before suddenly seemed insignificant or trivial. I had also learned to listen to my body and what my spirit wanted, to be more protective of my energy, and more discerning about the kind of people and energy I surrounded myself with. Finally, I gained deeper compassion and empathy for people who were suffering with health or trauma issues. It was as if

I had new vision and more sensory receptors.

Following my recovery, my spiritual path opened up even more. I became a deeper seeker and wanted to understand myself better and what I was here to learn. Interestingly enough, I started attracting many cancer patients and people with serious illnesses as Jikiden Reiki clients at my clinics. I could now speak with more authority on how holistic therapies and medicine could help them and, if they were interested, set them up with my team of practitioners.

In 2014, less than a year into my recovery, I also became a Jikiden Reiki teacher so I could share this remarkable therapy that served me so well during my own healing. I was passionate about teaching people Jikiden Reiki so they could learn to heal themselves and others.

It has now been seven years since the diagnosis and I can say wholeheartedly—I am thriving! I am still living with lymphoma, but doing so well that I often forget I have it. In fact, the cancer has been decreasing every year, much to the bewilderment of my doctors. I am in excellent health and living on purpose, doing work I love in service to others. I am living proof that holistic medicine and therapies can work, even for serious health issues like cancer.

None of us know when it's our time to go, but we always have power and agency when it comes to our health and life choices. The key is to learn to listen and follow our true voice rather than that of our ego. Not an easy thing, I know, but it's one of most the important things we can do to improve our lives, or, as in my case, save it.

ABOUT THE AUTHOR: Sanae Okada has been helping others through the healing arts since 2000. She uses a range of holistic therapies, including Jikiden Reiki®, Shiatsu and health and life coaching. Sanae is also a Jikiden Reiki Shihankaku Teacher and is registered with the Jikiden Reiki Institute of Japan and Canada. Through her wellness company, The Healing Lounge, Sanae and her team provide services to individuals and companies, including Microsoft Studios and Electronic Arts Canada. Sanae's personal clientele includes many celebrities such as musicians K'naan and

Maestro Fresh Wes and leading CEOs Hamed Shahbazi and Brian Paes-Braga. She is currently expanding her remote Jikiden Reiki services so she can help more people worldwide.

Sanae Okada
Jikiden Reiki Seminars
jikidenreikiseminars.com
info@jikidenreikiseminars.com

A Message from Green Tara
Kathy Sipple

Many of us dream of a better, safer, more caring world,
without recognizing that it all begins with creating and
maintaining a deeper love in our own home. The seeds of
world peace should be planted in our own backyard.
~ Anthon St. Maarten, Divine Living: The Essential Guide
To Your True Destiny

Spread Too Thin

It's a cold December day in Valparaiso, Indiana, yet I am warm beneath wonderful-smelling soft blankets on the massage table. "What brings you here?" my new massage therapist asks. I share the details of my recent car accident. A driver ran a red light and t-boned my SUV, leaving it totaled and me with a mess of paperwork as well as some pinched nerves, restricted neck movement, and pain. The silver lining: I finally replaced the destroyed vehicle with a used Prius—an eco-friendly move I had been wanting to make for several years.

Before the chaos of the accident settles, I lose my primary source of income as a corporate social media marketing trainer when the company that hires me files for bankruptcy. I enjoyed the work a lot at the beginning. Besides it paying well, it was a thrill to travel to distant cities and work in beautiful meeting rooms with interesting people. But keeping up with the demands of travel and all the changes in technology had become exhausting and I had begun to yearn for a simpler existence. A few full-time positions come up and parts of them sound good, but they're not fully me. A distant memory resurfaces—I remember telling my husband years ago that

I wanted to change my career focus in 2020—20/20, a new vision, a new me! I had been half-joking then, when 2020 seemed so very far away. Now 2020 is upon me and I don't feel ready. I don't know what's next but I know I need to hold out for work that makes me feel fully alive.

I love my part-time job as a Regional Resilience Coordinator with Earth Charter Indiana, but the one-year contracted position will be up in June. Reliant on grant-funding, their budget only allows for twenty hours monthly from me. Climate resilience is a huge job—much more than one person can handle in five hours a week! Luckily, I have met an incredible team of volunteers and together we host a Climate Action Blitz in February. It is very successful, attracting citizens from thirteen communities in Northwest Indiana and featuring lots of great speakers and presentations. Many new connections are made and vows taken, committing to contact local elected officials to encourage passing climate resolutions in their towns or cities. The success is bittersweet, though, for I know I need to find another job and will likely not be able to afford as much time working on environmental issues.

Green Tara's Message

I land an administrative part-time job to supplement my environmental work. I am not excited about it but rationalize that a bird in the hand is worth two in the bush. It's not in alignment with my skills or values, but it's only temporary. Since it doesn't begin until mid-March I decide to roadtrip to Cincinnati to visit my family. I sense my parents are worried about me; they sense I am not my usual enthusiastic self.

My mother is a gifted reiki healer; she offers me a treatment and I gladly accept. During my session I "see" a woman I recognize as the High Priestess from my tarot deck. She invites me to follow her behind a veil that covers the opening of her sacred temple. She guides me past other manifestations of the Divine Feminine until we arrive before a graceful serene woman who I only vaguely recognize. "Are you Tara?" I ask her. "I am Green Tara," she answers. "Earth needs you at this time for its healing. You must heal yourself as well. You must regain your sovereignty, free yourself to do the work that is needed. Time is of the essence. Do not be afraid."

I know very little about Green Tara prior to her "visit" but I quickly do some research online and am grateful for this meaningful experience. I excitedly share the message from Green Tara around the dinner table with family that night. A phone call from my worried husband disturbs the reverie. He tells me the first case of COVID-19 in Indiana has been reported and the governor is declaring a public health emergency. The next morning I drive the three-hundred-mile return trip without stopping, anxious to get back home.

Getting My House in Order

Kindness, respect, compassion, and encouragement are the compost tea of relationships—they feed all the beneficial impulses. When we respect one another's ideas, think well of one another's motives, and support one another's visions, we create a high-energy atmosphere in which creativity flourishes.
~ Starhawk

As March unfolds my calendar clears—the job I was to begin is on hold due to the pandemic. Likewise, a paid out-of-town speaking engagement and even the local Earth Day celebration I was supposed to emcee are canceled! No more massage or travel for a while…My life plans, along with the lives of many, are suspended indefinitely.

I connect with friends near and far via Zoom. My ego still wants me to plug into "big" things of international importance, to be the heroine who leaves her mark on the world and offers comfort in this time of adversity. The first few days I am glued to my screen, offering a listening ear to others who are struggling with the challenges of coronavirus and how to adapt.

I develop a headache that doesn't go away for weeks. Each time I try to return to online meetings my body rebels. I hear Green Tara's voice and she is telling me to go outside.

The weather is warming. I decide this unexpected downtime is the perfect opportunity to convert our front yard from a traditional lawn to native plants and raised bed gardens for flowers and food. If I do this, it will definitely be an outlier in my neighborhood of all traditional looking lawns so I seek input from neighbors via our Facebook group, sharing a rendering of my vision for the transformed yard and some of my reasons for wanting to do it: reduce or eliminate the need for mowing, allow for some food production, improve drainage for our yard and the surrounding area, and provide better habitat for pollinators. I am grateful and a bit surprised that no one objects—comments are neutral to positive. I proceed with sheet mulching, an ancient technique for converting grass to garden beds in preparation for the micro prairie I will install to replace our existing lawn.

Garden centers are closed due to the pandemic so I get creative about sourcing the materials I need. On trash pickup day I get up early to appropriate cardboard boxes my neighbors leave on the curb. Other friends offer me plant starts. I offer them homemade pizza and bread in return. The yard looks a mess as construction is underway but I have a beautiful vision and I see it taking shape. My body's flexibility is restored and I notice I am no longer in pain, just the regular muscle soreness from digging, bending, and lifting. I feel stronger and leaner. I sleep well at night.

By the end of May my native plants and heirloom vegetables are all planted, and I'm already noticing more diverse wildlife. I spot a bird I've never seen before—a Northern Flicker—in my yard. I also notice more hummingbirds than ever, along with lots of dragonflies, butterflies, and toads too. All of this new life at home in my yard brings me joy.

Social Climate

For centuries seekers have been looking for a holy place on Earth. They believe it is called Shambala and that in that place a connection can happen between anyone and the universal wisdom. ...And they will not find it if they keep searching this way, for Shambala is inside each of us, and its outward manifestation is recreated by people. ~ Anastasia via Vladimir Megre, The Dimension of Love

By July I'm enjoying the fruits of my labors—I sit outside in the shade of my trellised vining plants and read a book, occasionally waving hello to neighbors as they pass by. I offer a pepper to a young dad walking by with his two young boys in a stroller. Another neighbor brings me some of her homemade baklava and I give her some yellow squash as a thank you. Another neighbor tells me seeing our yard makes her happy every time she passes it; our conversation about the environment deepens and she asks me for resources so she can explore further. I am grateful my yard has become a space that connects me not only to wildlife and the Earth but also more to my neighbors, especially in a time that otherwise feels very socially isolating.

With the yard transformation complete and the temperatures getting too hot for intense outdoor labor, I yearn to return to purposeful, fulfilling work. Right on cue, my Executive Director at Earth Charter Indiana tells me they have secured funding that will enable me to continue for another year and to expand my role as well.

Buoyed by the show of support, I deepen my commitment to the environmental work with a team of incredibly intelligent, passionate volunteers. We meet weekly online and I find I never have headaches with this group and this work. I take it as my body's feedback that I am on the right path.

We name ourselves Northwest Indiana (NWI) Region Resilience and even create a logo, a website, and a social media presence. We decide on a shared aim—to facilitate a region-wide greenhouse gas emissions inventory to determine a baseline we can improve upon through future climate action plans. We reach out to staff from Indiana University's Environmental Resilience Institute. They tell us this has never been done in the state of Indiana and only a few times in the country. They attend our meetings and introduce us to helpful resources.

To succeed, we need buy-in from local cities, towns, counties, and the regional planning commission. It is a long process that involves reaching out to local elected officials and the regional planning commission. We start a petition to engage citizens and start a fundraiser too. In August the first of three counties and one town opt in. In September the second county and the regional planning commission gives its show of support at the committee level. The work is not complete—within me, my garden, or our climate work. All of it will always be work in progress, I realize. I order another truckload of mulch, looking forward to devoting time to preparing my beloved garden for the Fall and Winter. The world has not yet emerged from its collective chrysalis necessitated by coronavirus, but I am hopeful that a more beautiful cooperative world is possible.

I consider that "corona" means crown in Spanish. While I would never have wished coronavirus on anyone and grieve those who lost loved ones because of it, I can't help thinking that one consequence of experiencing it was regaining sovereignty over my own life.

What else is possible if we learn to work together more harmoniously, I wonder. For today, I am grateful for the butterflies drawing sustenance from flowers I have planted from seed. I'm grateful to wave to neighbors that were once acquaintances and now considered friends. I'm grateful for the gift I have been given through the work I am doing. I am grateful for the bountiful harvest of vegetables I gather for the evening meal. Tonight I will bake a loaf of homemade bread and open our first bottle of wine made with last year's grapes and I will toast to what lies ahead, like a Queen.

ABOUT THE AUTHOR: Kathy Sipple is available to help communities build resilience through social technology, climate action, timebanking, and permaculture. She is a Sociocracy Facilitator-in-training and is working on a book, *Healing Earth Together*, expected to be published in 2021. The book will serve as a guide for communities to address environmental and social justice issues while enriching the quality of life. Sipple holds a degree in Economics from the University of Michigan and is a member of Mensa. She lives in Valparaiso, Indiana—the "Vale of Paradise"—with her husband John and their black Lab Bodhi.

Kathy Sipple
kathysipple.com
linktr.ee/kathysipple
kathy@cothrive.org
219-405-9482

About the Authors

**Are you inspired by the stories in this book?
Let the authors know.**

**See the contact information at the end of each chapter
and reach out to them.**

They'd love to hear from you!

Author Rights & Disclaimer

Each author in this book retains the copyright and all inherent rights to their individual chapter. Their stories are printed herein with each author's permission.

Each author is responsible for the individual opinions expressed through their words. Powerful You! Publishing bears no responsibility for the content of the stories by these authors.

Acknowledgements & Gratitude

WHERE TO BEGIN? We have such deep gratitude for the beautiful individuals who enhance our lives. We're especially happy and grateful that our circle that continues to grow and for the gifts it bestows.

To the authors of this book, we honor, love, and admire you. Your openness with your stories exemplifies your passion for assisting others through their own transformation, and your personal resilience and courage light the way for us to be braver in our own lives. Thank you for sharing this journey with us. We are honored.

There are many beautiful souls who we gratefully call our tribe who offer their guidance, expertise, love, and support!

Our editor Dana Micheli – Your intuition, sense of humor, creativity, and willingness are exactly what we need to get to the heart of the stories. We appreciate our partnership and friendship, and we love you.

Our awesome training team, AmondaRose Igoe, Kathy Sipple, and Karen Flaherty – your caring hearts and vast expertise light the way for our authors. We love and appreciate each of you—more with each book!

Roe Couture DeSaro – You are the ultimate Gutsy Gal, enlightened spirit, wayshower, and friend. We are so very happy and grateful for your inspiration, your example, and our connection. We love you.

Our friends and families, we love you! You are always with us. We feel you in our hearts and appreciate the support, love, and lessons you provide for us. You've helped make us better humans.

Above all, we are grateful for the Divine Spirit that flows through us each day providing continued blessings, lessons, and opportunities for growth, peace and JOY!

Namaste` and Blessings, Love, and Gratitude,
Sue Urda and Kathy Fyler

About Sue Urda and Kathy Fyler

Sue and Kathy have been friends for 30 years and business partners since 1994. They have received many awards and accolades for their businesses over the years and continue to love the work they do and the people they do it with. As publishers, they are honored to help people share their stories, passions, and lessons.

Their mission is to raise the vibration of people and the planet and to connect and empower women in their lives. Their calling has been years in the making and is a gift from Spirit.

The strength of their partnership lies in their deep respect, love, and understanding of one another as well as their complementary skills and knowledge. Kathy is a technology enthusiast, web goddess, and free-thinker. Sue is an author and speaker with a love of creative undertakings. Their honor, love, and admiration for each other are boundless.

Together their energies combine to feed the flames of countless women who are seeking truth, empowerment, joy, peace, and connection with themselves, their own spirits, and other women.

Connect with Sue and Kathy:

Powerful You! Inc.
239-280-0111
info@powerfulyou.com
PowerfulYouPublishing.com
SueUrda.com

About Roe Couture DeSaro

Roe is a multi-award-winning entrepreneur, TEDx speaker, four-time bestselling author, transformational leader, influencer, coach, and facilitator of courageous conversations that move the needle. After breaking several glass ceilings for a high-ranking Wall Street firm, leading Stockbrokers to selling $100 million of an innovative product, she founded Gutsy Gals Get More, LLC. Her collective learning programs are uniquely experiential to help women uplevel their mindset, unleash their brilliance and step into their power so they can make a difference while earning wild money.

As a strong advocate for feminine/masculine balance, she has experienced women taking more risks and achieving more than they ever had before gracefully. She created a world where females have their voice respected, because she learned how to do it herself.

Roe touches a chord, spiritually, intellectually, and emotionally. Under her leadership and coaching, breakthroughs occur, and her Gutsy Gal gatherings are sold-out. Today she loves mentoring 'Women Leaders' to build successful businesses and careers.

Connect with Roe:
Roe@RoeCoutureDesaro.com
GutsyGalsGetMore.com
732-962-6052
Facebook.com/beagutsygal
Facebook.com/groups/GutsyGalsGetMore

Powerful You! Publishing
Sharing Wisdom ~ Shining Light

Are You Called to be an Author?

If you're like most people, you may find the prospect of writing a book daunting. Where to begin? How to proceed? No worries! We're here to help.

Whether you choose to contribute to an anthology or write your own book, we're here for you. We'll be your guiding light, professional consultant, and enthusiastic supporter. If you see yourself as an author partnering with a publishing company who has your best interest at heart and expertise to back it up, we'd be honored to be your publisher.

We provide personalized guidance through the writing and editing process, as well as many necessary tools for your success as an author. We offer complete publishing packages and our service is designed for a personal and optimal author experience.

We are committed to helping individuals express their voice and shine their light into the world. Are you ready to start your journey as an author? Do it with Powerful You! Publishing.

Powerful You! Publishing
239-280-0111
powerfulyoupublishing.com

Anthology Books

Empowering Transformations for Women
Women Living Consciously
Journey to Joy
Pathways to Vibrant Health & Well-Being
Women Living Consciously Book II
Healthy, Abundant, and Wise
Keys to Conscious Business Growth
The Gifts of Grace & Gratitude
Heal Thy Self
Empower Your Life
Heart & Soul
The Beauty of Authenticity
WOKE

Other Books

Powerful Intentions, Everyday Gratitude - Books I & II
Let Me Walk the Journey with You
Medicine Jewelry – Working with Rock People
Led By Purpose
Divinely Fit
A Journey Back to Restoration
Seven Sundays to Sweet Inner Serenity
Live Beyond Your Loss
Frankie: My Brother, My Hero
The Power of Love and Awakened Consciousness
Drowning in Silence
It Is Well
Manage Your Life ~ Master Your Stress

TRANSFORMATION
is an evolutionary process.

Be Gentle with Yourself.